"In most financial books, the author would never do what Howard has done: recount with unflinching honesty the big financial mistakes he and his subscribers have made over the years so readers can avoid the same stumbling blocks and pitfalls. Only a very secure man would have the guts to do that."

—Robert Allen, Author of Nothi—— —wn

"I love Howard's old-fashioned moral p~~
—Mark Skousen, E(

"His mega-bestseller, 'How to Prosper L   ..a Years,'
changed millions of lives in the late '70s.'
—John Mauldin, Author of Bulls Eye Investing

"What I like about Howard is he's very principled, you don't have to figure out what his principles are. He says what he thinks is right. And he's very effective."

—James Hansen, Former Utah Congressman

"Besides containing excellent investment advice (I made over 60% on the most recent recommendation that I followed), he teaches more real world economics than any of the economics textbooks that I used in my classes during the last 40 years."

—R. Clites, Economics professor, Milligan College , TN

"In my opinion, Howard Ruff comes up with more economic insights in a single week than most economists come up with in a lifetime."

—William E. Simon, former Secretary of the Treasury

"Howard Ruff finally takes the "con" out of economics. He is not only one of the most interesting observers of our economic system and what makes it tick, he writes about it in his own no-nonsense manner, which every working man and woman can appreciate and understand."

—Howard Jarvis, father of California's famous Proposition 13

About the Author

Howard Ruff has been a fixture in the financial-advice world for 34 years. His book *How to Prosper During the Coming Bad Years,* published in 1977, is still the world champion. It is the biggest-selling financial book in history with over 2.6 million copies sold and was on the top of the New York Times best-seller list for two years in both hard cover and paperback.

His newsletter, *The Ruff Times*, has had over 600,000 subscribers and counting.

Howard says he won't retire until he has to be hauled off the field of battle on his shield. He sometimes complains, "I have a 35 year-old brain in a 78 year-old body," and he has never lost his interest in following the financial world and the politics that underlies it.

Howard has been a charming and engaging fixture on every major talk show, including Oprah, Good Morning America, the Today Show, Regis and Kathy Lee, Donahue, NightLine, Wall Street Week, Crossfire, and others – often multiple times.

He's a maverick who often strays from the usual Wall-Street crowd.

HOW TO
PROSPER
IN THE AGE OF
OBAMANOMICS

HOW TO
PROSPER
IN THE AGE OF
OBAMANOMICS

A RUFF PLAN FOR
HARD TIMES AHEAD

Howard J. Ruff

Saratoga
Publishing
Orem, Utah

Saratoga
Publishing

Saratoga Publishing
51 West Center, Suite 519
Orem, UT 84057

Publishers Cataloguing-in-Publication Data

Ruff, Howard J.

    How to prosper in the age of Obamanomics : a Ruff plan for hard times ahead / Howard J. Ruff. -- 1st ed. -- Orem, UT : Saratoga Publishers, c2009.

    p. ; cm.

    ISBN: 978-0-9842713-0-6

    1. United States--Economic conditions. 2. Inflation (Finance)
3. Finance, Personal. 4. Investments.
    I. Title.

HG179 .R74 2009   2009909983
332.024--dc22   0912

Printed in the United States of America on Acid-Free Paper

First Edition

Book Design: Ghislain Viau
Photo of the Author: Aaron Nielsen
Book Consultant: Ellen Reid

Table Of Contents

Part I—America's Current Economic Mess

Part II—On the Horizon:
The Economic Storm of the Century

Part III—Prescriptions

Foreword
ABOUT THE AUTHOR, BY THE AUTHOR

Life's tragedy is that we get old too soon and wise too late.
—Benjamin Franklin

I f you are going to listen to my ideas, you have every right to know what kind of a guy I am. I thought a little bit of history might be appropriate—and hopefully enjoyable.

To begin, I can't resist reprinting here something I wrote just for fun many years ago. We'd just had a neighborhood barbecue where we played a game recounting things we had done that we thought nobody else had. It was a fun trip down memory lane and it started my memory running wild. My life has been so full and unusual that at times it amazes even me. I just had to write it all down to share with you. Enjoy!

* * * *

A Trip Down Memory Lane

- My 1978 book and my newsletter, The Ruff Times helped sustain the great gold and silver bull market of the 1970s, and I made several hundred percent for my subscribers in the metals! That was my first financial home run.

- I once gave one spool of eight-pound-test monofilament fishing line to the chief of a village in the Amazon jungle in return for two monkey-skull necklaces, a blow gun and darts, a bow and arrows and an anaconda snake skin. And, after consulting with Kay, I respectfully declined the chief's offer of a night with one of his four wives (they smelled terrible) in return for a second spool.

- I've walked through the dramatic story of the death of Rasputin, the Mad Monk, right on the actual murder scene in a restored palace in Leningrad.

- I've interviewed (with Jack Anderson) newly elected President Havel of Czechoslovakia in Prague Palace while he was wearing Nike shoes and a UCLA Bruins sweatshirt. He had been a political prisoner until the Iron Curtain went down.

- I've visited the Forbidden City and the Great Wall in China, Machu Pichu, the Imperial Palace in Bangkok, wild-game preserves in Kenya and South Africa, snorkeled on the Great Barrier Reef, and watched great sea turtles lay their eggs and baby turtles hatch.

- Ollie North, my Washington staff, and I persuaded Ronald Reagan to send Stinger missiles to the Afghan Freedom Fighters, which bogged down the Soviet army in Afghanistan for six years, which led to Soviet bankruptcy, which led to Gorbachev withdrawing Russian financial and military support from Eastern Europe, Cuba and Nicaragua, which led to a break-out of freedom, which led to the crash of the Iron Curtain.

- I have sung as a featured artist with the Mormon Tabernacle Choir, the Philadelphia Orchestra, the National Symphony, and on the Ed Sullivan Show. I've also performed in, conducted, or directed hundreds of performances of Gilbert and Sullivan operas and became deeply involved with the Utah Lyric Opera society as a performer, director, conductor, and General Manager. I was a church choir director at age sixteen.

- I had my own national TV talk show and daily two-minute radio commentary in more than three hundred markets.

- I was called a liar in an angry speech on the floor of Congress by Congressman Neal of South Carolina and was denounced by Pravda, Tass, and Soviet-controlled radio Kabul as a right-wing "radical reactionary."

- I once refused a phone call from an angry President Ronald Reagan. He swore at me, and then two weeks later sent me an unsolicited, personally autographed portrait as a peace offering. It hangs in my office.

- A ruffled Jimmy Carter succeeded in knocking fifty stations off my radio syndicate by threatening them with trouble at license-renewal time if they didn't cancel my show.

- I married a celestial woman, Kay. We've been through thick and thin (I used to be thin) for fifty-four years, probably because we have one thing in common: we're both in love with the same man!

- We have given birth to nine children, adopted four teenagers and one adult, and helped raise eighteen foster children—and endured the heart-breaking death of one child.

- I broke up an orphanage run by American pedophiles in Bangkok, which resulted in jailing them and caused an international incident between ABC, me, and the Thai government. I set up my own orphanage in Bangkok to take care of the children.

- I've been on Donahue, Good Morning America, The Today Show, Merv Griffin, Dinah Shore, Oprah, Regis and Kathy Lee, Crossfire, PBS Late Night, Nightline, Charlie Rose, McNeil-Lehrer, Wall Street Week, and hundreds of local radio and TV talk shows, many of them multiple times.

- I have had dinner with Chiang Kai-shek and Madame Chiang, the Secretary to the King of Denmark, and President Synghman Rhee, the Father of modern Korea.

- I sang the Star Spangled Banner at the White House numerous times as a soloist for the Air Force Band and Singing Sergeants where I served as soloist and announcer for four years.

- I sold one hundred thousand copies of an album, *Howard Ruff Sings*, with the Osmond brothers and the BYU Philharmonic and A Cappella Choir as my backup groups.

- I caught a piranha in the Amazon and ate it (poetic justice?). It tasted like a bluegill.

- I've owned nine airplanes, and have logged three thousand, five hundred hours as "pilot in command."

- I was forced into bankruptcy in 1968 by a newspaper strike and then paid off half a million dollars (plus interest) in debts from which I had been legally discharged. It took me twelve years.

- Evelyn Wood personally taught me to read three thousand words per minute, and I then developed the marketing and advertising that made her famous.

- I cruised the Mediterranean with Art Linkletter.

- I took over Madame Tussaud's Wax Works in London one night for a private party for my subscribers, and Kay and I flew to Ireland just to spend a weekend in a castle with Elizabeth Taylor. Unfortunately, she didn't show, so we spent a weekend in a castle in Ireland *without* Elizabeth Taylor.

- Whenever I think I've accomplished a lot, I just remind myself that when Mozart was my age—he'd been dead for forty years.

* * * *

My Childhood

I was born with a wooden spoon in my mouth. My mother was widowed when I was only six months old. We were poor but I didn't know it, because in the depths of the Great Depression everybody else was poor too. We were actually too poor to afford a father. My Mom literally took in sewing to feed my eleven-years-older brother Jim and me. By the time I was nine years old, I knew what I wanted to be when I grew up: a writer? a financial advisor? a Prophet of Doom? None of the above! I was a really good boy soprano, and I knew I wanted to be a singer on Broadway or at the Met someday.

When I was a pre-adolescent during World War II, we lived in Reno, Nevada, and I became a member of the Victory Boys, a group of boy sopranos. We gave patriotic programs all over the state of Nevada. That's when I found what I loved the most in the whole world—applause!!

When I was thirteen, we moved back to Oakland where my voice changed abruptly from soprano to baritone. So at age sixteen, I joined a San Francisco musical-theatre company and a year or two later sang in San Francisco's famous opera clubs for ten dollars a night plus tips. We would sing operatic arias and duets by request from 9:00 p.m. to 2:00 a.m. It was really just a smoke-filled bar, but I was doing what I loved to do.

Young Adulthood

When I was eighteen, my voice teacher told me she had arranged for a full-ride scholarship to the Curtis School of Music in Philadelphia. Curtis was considered on a par with Julliard, and could be a very important step on my road to the Met, but when I told my Mom, she threw a big monkey wrench into the works: "But you are supposed to go on a mission!" As a practicing Mormon family, it was expected that young men would volunteer to leave home for two years and teach the gospel to potential converts, and I didn't want to go because I knew that my Curtis scholarship would be toast.

After a period of intense spiritual inquiry, I finally made the hard decision that unbeknownst to me would change the whole direction of my personal and professional life. I decided that if I served the Lord, He would take care of me. So with blind faith, I launched out into the dark and decided on the mission. They sent me to the heathens— Washington D.C.—and not only did it jump-start my lifelong interest in government, economics and politics, but it was there that I first heard the Air Force Band and Singing Sergeants in a Sunday night concert on the Capitol steps. It would change my life forever. I was also befriended by the two current Utah senators (Arthur Watkins and Wallace Bennett, the father of Utah's present senator), as well as J. Willard Marriott, Sr. of hotel fame. We had had long discussions about life, business, and the issues of the day, and I began forming my economic, business and political opinions.

I attended the Missionary School of Hard Knocks—on thousands of doors —and learned one of the great lessons of life that every salesman and marketer must learn: how to live with continuous rejection and failure and keep bouncing back day after day. It was a tough but immensely satisfying and character-building experience, and I regretted it coming to an end.

After my mission, I went to BYU to continue my musical education. When I ran out of money after my junior year, I went back to San Francisco where my mother now lived, to make some money so I could go back to school, singing in the opera clubs by night and selling Chryslers by day. Then, unexpectedly, I was reclassified 1-A in the draft and ordered to report for induction into the army. I remembered the Air Force Singing Sergeants, called the Pentagon to get their phone number in Washington D.C., and was given the number of Colonel George S. Howard, Chief of Bands and Music for the Air Force. I called him. He told me he had an opening for a new baritone soloist, but wouldn't be in California to audition me for six months, so I told him, "I'll audition in Washington next Wednesday."

The Singing Sergeants and Marriage

I borrowed $150 from my big brother, flew to Washington, auditioned, got the job (with a letter to prove it!), and enlisted in the Air Force. After only three weeks of basic training, I was ordered to report to Washington to go with the Air Force Symphony on a tour of Iceland and Scandinavia as soloist and announcer. I called the lovely Kay Felt in San Francisco and rather arrogantly informed her we would be married in Salt Lake City on the way to Washington the following Monday.

Fortunately, she couldn't think of any good reason why not, so we were married on schedule. Kay Felt became Kay Felt Ruff (when she realized what her name would be, it almost killed the marriage). She has been the spiritual and nurturing center of my life and family, and our numerous kids and grandkids all adore her—and so do I.

I traveled all over the world with the band, meeting and in some cases having dinner with historical figures and assorted prime ministers and royalty on three continents and twenty countries We also toured in forty-nine states. I was having an amazing educational experience, while Kay was at home having babies.

But I wasn't really an absentee father. Being a Singing Sergeant was a government job. When we weren't on tour (we were only gone about fifteen weeks out of the year), we only had to report to rehearsals for two hours a day, so I got a job with a stock broker, continuing my economic and financial education, and spent a lot of time at home, helping Kay with the kids and learning to love fatherhood.

My First Business Career

When my four-year hitch was up, we moved to Denver to work for my broker/employer, stumbled across Evelyn Wood Reading Dynamics, bought the Denver franchise, then the Bay Area franchise, and launched my business career: teaching the world to read faster and more efficiently. I learned I had valuable gifts as a marketer, writer, and public speaker, but I was also laying the foundation for my first big Learning Experience—a business failure!

We'd had eight glorious years, with more than 10,000 students in the San Francisco Bay area, and I wrote the ads and designed the marketing for all the nationwide franchises. I became the protégé of Evelyn Wood, who taught me how to read over three thousand words-per-minute, a life-changing skill that has served me well ever since. We taught University of California and Stanford law students, high school and junior-high students, and businessmen how to read more rapidly and efficiently and also enjoy and absorb more from their reading. As the money was rolling in, we spent it. We gave money to the Oakland Symphony, and I bought Kay a $1,000 designer dress so that when we had our picture on the society page at post-concert receptions, she would look great. In the meantime, our family was continuing to grow, and Kay bore more much-loved and much-wanted children.

However, I was making the biggest mistake of my life to that date, (although bigger mistakes would come later). Because I thought the gravy train would last forever, we didn't bother to accumulate any savings or cash reserves. We had good credit and used it. We spent our money as if there were no tomorrow, or, to be more accurate, I did. Kay expressed her concerns, which I discounted because I thought I knew better.

Then disaster struck. I had planned an eight-page advertising supplement to go into all of the Bay Area newspapers one Sunday. On Friday night a wildcat strike hit all the Bay Area papers, and the Sunday paper was never published. I had spent $25,000 printing that supplement, which at the time seemed like all the money in the world. We couldn't just keep the inserts and use them at a later time because they were all geared toward specific demonstration meetings on specific dates at specific places all over the Bay Area.

I was in deep trouble. I didn't have any cash reserves, accounts payable began to pile up, we were up to our ears in hock and personal debt, and I was in arrears with my royalties. Finally, the parent company, seeing an opportunity to grab off the business and resell it to someone else, abruptly cancelled my franchise and notified the sheriff. My doors were locked, and I was out of business. I went to work rich (I thought) and came home broke. It ruined my whole day.

Learning From a Failure

This forced me into bankruptcy, but Kay and I, prompted by some ethical counseling by local church leaders, decided that even though we had filed bankruptcy, legally discharging half-a-million dollars in debt, we would not be right with our creditors and the Lord if we didn't someday pay it off. So I made perhaps the most important decision of my life—I would eventually pay off those debts. This meant I couldn't just get a J.O.B.; I had to become rich—again.

That all happened in October 1968, and we had already been hit by a tragedy the previous June when our toddler, Ivan, was drowned in our swimming pool. It was a devastating year, but I now know that sometimes the healing and correcting spirit of God can only enter us through gaping wounds. This spiritual process had begun at Ivan's death when we had to decide what we really believed. We were ready to make the spiritual, financial, and emotional commitment to pay off half a million dollars in debt. It took us twelve years to pay for that dead horse, but we did it!

In the meantime, we had taken in a teenaged foster son in the neighborhood who had become estranged from his family. The word got around, so over the following years we took in more than eighteen of them, mostly teenagers, for varying lengths of time. We eventually adopted five.

A Business Comeback and a New Perspective

I began my business comeback as a distributor in the multi-level sales organization for a major manufacturer of food supplements called The Neo Life Company. It's still in existence today and is one of the honorable survivors in the multi-level-marketing business. I quickly became its largest distributor and won all of the company awards for performance. This began a lifelong obsession with keeping up with the research and development of nutritional supplements.

About this time, I began to worry about what I saw as a coming train wreck for the economy.

When I was in an airport, I saw a book whose title intrigued me, *How to Prepare for the Coming Crash* by Robert Preston. Thinking it was a way to stay safe if the airplane went down, I bought it to read on the plane, but that wasn't the crash it was talking about. Preston advocated investing in silver and gold as a hedge against an inflation-induced economic crash. For the first time, my stock-market-oriented brain began to turn in that direction. I began to study the fundamentals of Austrian economics and the inflation that would lead to economic troubles and a resurgence of gold and silver. I began to worry about what I believed the government was doing to the economy with its inflationary policies.

I also became convinced that there was a real possibility of a deep recession that could turn into a depression, characterized by high inflation and unemployment. I became a vocal advocate of emergency food-storage as a kind of family-insurance program. After all, we had once lived on our stored food when the bottom had dropped out of our financial lives in 1968. This traditional Mormon practice grew not so much out of its theology as it did out of its nineteenth-century pioneer self-sufficiency culture. It was not an apocalyptic practice, but a very practical one, designed for just the kind of circumstances we had to face. This very prudent, riskless piece of financial advice planted the roots of what would someday be the cause of my near-universal bad press.

I wrote my first book, a very bad self-published book called *Famine and Survival in America,* not realizing how powerful words could be. Rather than a carefully reasoned discussion of why you ought to have a food-storage program as a conservative, prudent precaution against hard times for your family, it sounded more like a scream in the night. But to my amazement, as I began to do radio and TV shows to promote this self-published book, it caught on as people were scared of what was happening in the world around them as inflation soared.

Riding High through Ruff Times

In the book, I promised to send a monthly update on the markets to book buyers, so I soon was sending out 5,000 monthly updates and going broke doing it. I sold off my supplement distributorship to finance a for-pay newsletter, which I called *The Ruff Times* to a chorus of sardonic jeers. My guts told me that name was right for the times. I launched *The Ruff Times* newsletter in June 1975, forecasting rising inflation, a falling stock market, and rising gold and silver prices. Was

I ever right! At the time, gold was only $105 an ounce and silver was under $2. They had not yet begun the spectacular bull market that would take them to $850 and $50 respectively.

As the precious metals and *The Ruff Times* took off, I decided I needed to write a manual for new subscribers because I couldn't reinvent the wheel every time I went to press. With no intention to publish it as anything but a manual, I wrote *How to Prosper During the Coming Bad Years*. A member of my board of directors knew many New York publishers, so he persuaded me to go there to meet several of them. Four of them wanted to publish the book. I chose Times Books, a division of the New York Times of all things. Tom Lipscomb, the president, was a brilliant publisher and marketer who believed passionately in me as well as the book, and he shared my philosophy. He and I made publishing history together—2.6 million copies!

By this time, I had a syndicated TV talk show called RUFFHOU$E, interviewing a lot of interesting guests. I got a call from a radio syndicator who had been distributing the Ronald Reagan daily radio commentary. When Reagan decided to run for President, he gave up his radio show, so they asked me to fill that slot, as I was getting a lot of notoriety as the book hit the top of the New York Times best-seller list and my TV show was gathering millions of viewers.

So I created a two-minute daily radio commentary, which eventually was on some three hundred stations. *The Ruff Times* was on its way to the stratosphere—or so I thought!

As a public service to benefit from my high profile and high levels of trust from my like-minded subscribers, I founded RuffPAC, a political action committee, and Free The Eagle, a registered lobby in Washington D.C. I began to fight for free-market issues and free-market-oriented candidates for public office. We were successful in some pretty important things. I previously mentioned how we persuaded President Reagan to get stinger missiles to the Afghan rebels. This forced the Soviets to fly so high they couldn't devastate the villages that were harboring the Mujahadin. It stalemated the war. When the body bags kept going home and the Soviet Union was on the verge of bankruptcy trying to support their functional equivalent of our Vietnam, eventually Gorbachev withdrew from Afghanistan, pulled back the Soviet Army from their Iron Curtain satellites, stopped their financial support of Cuba, the Sandinistas in Nicaragua, and communist insurgents in Africa, and the Iron Curtain began to crumble. I honestly believe we had something to do with starting that whole process.

In any event, *The Ruff Times* had become a publishing phenomenon. *How to Prosper During the Coming Bad Years* was Number One or Number Two on the hardcover best-seller list for months, and when the paperback came out a year later, it not only stayed at or near the top of the hardcover list, but was also Number One on the paperback list. It stayed high on both lists for two years.

Early on, "the Prophet (sometimes spelled *Profit* by the media) of Doom" title began to plague me. It seems that hardcore "survivalists" were getting a lot of media attention. These extremists shared some of my economic views (gold, silver, stored food, etc.), but they believed that society would collapse completely, so they were building impregnable retreats in the mountains and buying lots of guns and storing food and hunkering down, waiting for the end. I had a chapter in *How to Prosper During the Coming Bad Years* about the advisability of a food-storage program as a riskless, prudent hedge against personal or public financial difficulties, and a lot of information on how to invest in gold and silver. There it was: guilt by association!

The simple-minded media saw me as a hook for critical stories about hardcore survivalists, and the Prophet of Doom title was forever attached to me, despite my protests. Heck, the "How to Prosper," in the title (which is not exactly an end-of-the-world idea) should have been a clue to them that they were wrong, but to no avail.

Way back in 1975 when I started publishing *The Ruff Times*, I foresaw the coming inflation that plagued us for the next seven years, and analyzed—correctly—that it would cause a big boom in gold and silver. I recommended gold when it was only $105 an ounce and silver when it was under $2. Gold subsequently went to $850 and silver to $50 for a few days. I published a sell order in 1980 when gold was $750 and silver at $35. This angered and offended my subscriber base, which now were mostly gold bugs, and they began deserting me as an apostate from the true religion of The Golden Calf. For twenty-two subsequent years, gold stayed below $300 and silver under $5.

I turned bullish on the stock market in 1983, mostly because of Ronald Reagan, and stayed bullish for several years. We did very well for my subscribers, but I started telling people to get out of the stock market about six months before it peaked in March 2000 and called the market an "unsustainable mania and a bubble." This was right on the money, as March 2000 was the peak of the greatest bull market in history and the beginning of the greatest bear market in history. I've been on the right side of that market ever since, keeping people out of it, and instead recommending thirty-year T-bonds and ten-year T-notes, where we had big profits in 2000-2003, and saved subscribers untold millions of dollars.

In 1983 I was at the top of my popularity. My book had become the biggest financial bestseller of all time. My syndicated TV show, RUFFHOU$E, and my daily radio commentary were popular across the nation. My newsletter, *The Ruff Times*, had more than 175,000 subscribers, and I thought I was a marketing genius, as all the direct-mail pieces I wrote worked. Because my Washington lobby, Free the Eagle, and RuffPAC, my Political Action Committee, were real powers in Washington, I had access to President Reagan and any senator and congressman I wanted. I was famous, I was rich, and the world was my oyster.

On the Downside

In retrospect, that was the high-water mark of my professional and business life. It would be all downhill business-wise from there. Little did I realize that I wasn't the marketing genius I thought I was. I was just a very lucky guy with the right message at the right time, and if conditions changed much, I wouldn't be so smart. Conditions changed!

Ironically, even though I had campaigned vigorously for him and had warm personal relations with him, the election of Ronald Reagan was the beginning of a long, downhill slide for me. I had made my mark in the world by telling people how to prosper during the scary Jimmy Carter-induced inflation of the 1970s. Ronald Reagan was my friend, and Jimmy Carter was my foil. Ronald Reagan and Paul Volcker's successful assault on the runaway inflation and interest rates of the late '70s made people less convinced we were facing some "Coming Bad Years," and properly so. My old message was less compelling. As I changed with the times and became properly bullish on America, the new message was less interesting than the old one, and media publicity was harder to come by.

During that years-long downhill slide, I made a series of stupid mistakes that taught me most of what I know today. I had learned how to make a fortune and had done it twice: once in good times and once in bad. Also, I had learned how to *lose* a fortune, and had done that twice—also in good times and bad.

In retrospect, as I became a celebrity, my financial success and notoriety infected me with a bad case of *hubris*—the Greek word for the arrogant pride of the gods. I unconsciously believed that I was so smart I could violate my own published rules with impunity and avoid the problems that would trip up lesser mortals, and my success wasn't teaching me a thing. Too often my operative principle was "do as I say, not as I do." Unfortunately, I was wrong—*really* wrong—and it has cost me millions. Much of what I thought I knew (that eventually turned out to be wrong) came out of my successes.

One reason I felt driven to write this sometimes embarrassing treatise is that I don't want my posterity to repeat my foolish mistakes; my successes are nowhere near as instructive and helpful. If I can't pass on what I learned about the things that no longer work—or didn't work in the first place—some of my most valuable experiences would be wasted. Making the mistakes I made will prevent them from becoming safely prosperous or really rich. I also want the cathartic benefit of publicly facing reality about myself and cramming a little humility down my unwilling throat. It will be too late when I am trying to explain my arrogant pride to God.

My Y2K Flop

I believed Y2K was a deadly serious threat that could have devastating effects on the economy. I said so in my newsletter, and even wrote a book on the subject. I was dead right about the seriousness of the problem, but for the only time in my life, I underestimated the willingness and the ability of government and industry to solve the problem in time to beat the deadline of January 1, 2000. Miraculously, they did fix it in time, due to the efforts of Senator Bob Bennett of Utah and others. On New Year's Day, 2000, when the dire consequences failed to materialize, I had egg all over my face, and that book became a big publishing flop. It wasn't that I had not analyzed the problem properly; it was that I didn't believe that they would have the will and the smarts to fix it in time. I was wrong. Big time!

Old Fogy Wisdom

This book could only be written by someone of my ripe years (sometimes I wish I was seventy-seven again). I've been observing the world of money through three serious recessions; three major bull and bear markets, including the late, lamented dot-com bubble of 1996-2000; the insane inflation of the 1970's; a real-estate boom and bust; a historic gold bull market and subsequent collapse; and thirteen children (five were adopted), eighteen foster children, seventy-six grandchildren, and eight great grandchildren. I've made and lost two fortunes by making some stupid pride-driven mistakes and been written off by Wall Street as a fringe character at times, but for a few glory years, I couldn't walk down any sidewalk in the Wall Street financial district without being recognized. For the last decade, I've been laying low, laboring away in relative obscurity just publishing my newsletter on the Internet, and waiting for gold's inevitable comeback. My patience has finally been rewarded; thence this book.

A Real Adult: I've Been There

I have been publishing *The Ruff Times* through thirty-four years of bull and bear markets in the precious metals. I've been around a long time, unlike most of the hot financial advisors and brokers today who weren't even born when I was already accurately predicting the markets. These big shots were the Invincible Optimists at the peak of the last bull market on Wall Street in the spring of 2000, and I was yelling at them (they didn't listen) to get out of the stock market. I think I am one of a handful of real adults in the Wall Street kindergarten with a long-range view of the world of money and an encyclopedic view of gold and silver.

In short, in a financial world that has been dominated by 20- and 30-something kids who weren't even stockbrokers during the last bear market in 1987, I'm one of a small clique of *real adults*— newsletter writers, financial publishers, analysts, and advisors—who have been around since the '60s and '70s and through the gold and silver bull market of the '70s. For the most part, Wall Street has not respected us. But that's okay because we don't have a lot of respect for many of them either.

If this book doesn't convince you to trust me, then I'm sorry. I tried.

Step One

Consider this book to be **the first step**, the jumping-off point, in your Ruffonomics education. Don't let it be the last. In order to make the best financial decisions, you'll need to keep learning.

No book stays right forever. In fact anyone who listens to me on TV, reads my books, and then follows my advice without keeping up with my ongoing commentaries could make some serious mistakes because things change at hyper-speed these days.

I can't stress enough that after you have read this book and understand the basics, things *will* change. My first big book, *How to Prosper During the Coming Bad Years*, is still fundamentally sound, so when I reissued it in 2007 as *How to Prosper During the Coming Bad Years in the 21ˢᵗ Century*, it was current and up-to-date. But the unprecedented events of the last two years have rapidly overtaken it. It's not current enough to be a safe day-to-day guide today, although it's still basically correct.

In order to keep up, I issue an eight-page newsletter (*The Ruff Times*) every three weeks as well as brief commentaries between issues. This is where you'll find your on-going Ruffonomics lessons and my interpretation of current economic events. It's the only way *not* to get left behind.

Please visit my website (www.rufftimes.com) to learn more about keeping your economic strategies up-to-date with a subscription to *The Ruff Times*.

Introduction

Coming Attractions

In this book:

- I hope to convince you that **Obamanomics is a near-fatal threat to prosperity** and a certain cause of hyperinflation**.**

- Further, I hope to convince you to adopt Ruffonomics—a unique set of strategies for families to make and keep money. If I can't convince the world to abandon Obamanomics, I *can* show families how to conduct their financial lives so they can make it through these difficult times.

- I will explain why **Obamanomics is the sure road to socialism**. You *must* understand what's happening in order to arm yourself against the onslaught of galloping socialism.

- I will tell you how and **why the American and global economies fell apart** in days.

- I will explain how **real optimists can make money during hard times**, regardless of politics, the markets, or the economy. There is always a silver lining, and more often than not, conventional wisdom misses it completely. In the coming years, the mavericks that leave the Wall Street herd will make most of the money.

- I will write with *you* **in mind**. I always write in terms that any average high school graduate can understand. Wall Street jargon has no place in my books or *The Ruff Times*, because the average person wouldn't understand it, would be turned off by it, and wouldn't follow such complicated advice anyway. I won't tell government or financial experts what to do (they wouldn't listen to me anyway), but I will tell *you* what to prepare for.

- I will explain why **traditional moral principles** are the foundation to everything I write about economics and investments. Investment decisions must be made in the context of the society in which we live. Traditional morality helped form this successful American society. Threats to that moral base make investing and family stability difficult, if not impossible. In Chapters Four and Seven, I will unveil the assault on your traditional family that has been orchestrated by Obama and other sexual anarchists. I'll show you why it matters economically.

- I will show you how **Political Economics** helps you know what to do with your money. The government spends more than forty percent of our Gross Domestic Product (GDP). What government does with that whopping amount of money *will* affect your life and your financial decisions. Just as generals always fight the last war, investment advisors usually respond to the last crisis and are immensely influenced by government policy. The political economy will always be an important part of what I write about in my books and in *The Ruff Times*. To ignore the political environment while making financial decisions is a fool's errand.

- I will explain the importance of **protecting and defending time-honored ideas** such as freedom, constitutional government, capitalism, entrepreneurism, and personal responsibility—including the right to succeed and keep the fruits of your labors. America was built by people who took calculated business risks and sometimes failed, but then picked themselves up, plunged into the battle again, and learned from the experience.

PART I
AMERICA'S CURRENT ECONOMIC MESS

CHAPTER 1

"We Have Seen The Enemy, And He Is Us" (Pogo):

OR HOW A SOCIALIST BOILS A FROG

There is danger from all men.
The only maxim of a free government
ought to be to trust no man living
with power to endanger the public liberty.
—John Adams

Remember the old adage that the only way to boil a frog is to *not* put him in boiling water because he will jump out? Instead, put him in lukewarm water and gradually turn up the heat. He'll be cooked before he even knows it.

Little by little, ever so subtly, the heat has been turned up in America, which is now near boiling. The water is getting painfully hotter by the minute and most Americans, like the duped frog, don't have a clue what's happening.

Ignorance

I'm constantly appalled at the ignorance of the American people. I hear it all the time when I take calls on radio talk show interviews. Just listen to Sean Hannity's weekly "Man on the Street" and you'll hear for yourself what I mean.

America is abounding in ignorance. Thomas Jefferson said: "If a nation expects to be ignorant and free in a state of civilization, it expects what never was and never will be."

The general public has no idea what they are doing on Election Day. All they know is that if they vote one way they will get benefits from government, and if they vote another way, they won't get as much.

America's youngest and allegedly brightest are completely ignorant of economic reality, traditional values, and investment truth. A recent Rasmussen poll conducted in April 2009 found only fifty-three percent of the country prefers capitalism to socialism. The remaining forty-seven percent of Americans (mostly young) either said they prefer socialism to capitalism or are undecided about which is better. In reality, they don't have the slightest idea what either word really means. They're slowly being cooked by their own ignorance.

Election by Ignorance

The monster vote that projected Barack Obama into the White House is a sorry case of ignorance in action. He is the least-experienced president who has ever been elected. His total political career consists of being a state legislator and a neighborhood activist, with only two years in the Senate, most of which time he spent campaigning for the presidency.

His lack of seasoning is one thing, but his life-long association with left-wing radicals and ties to corrupt, extreme leftist groups like ACORN is utterly chilling.

You'd expect a man entrusted with the largest free-market economy in the world to know something about capitalism, but in fact, Obama's knowledge of economics and free-market capitalism is literally appalling. He has said himself that as a college student, he sought out mentoring by Marxist professors.

Obama certainly is an attractive and talented young man. He is a brilliant speaker (when he has a teleprompter), has a beautiful wife, two lovely children, and all the outward appearances that made him an ideal candidate. But those aren't adequate reasons to make him the leader of the free world!

Tragically, charisma and eloquence seem to be the only criteria uninformed voters care about.

Now he is turning up the heat. America is rapidly becoming a boiled frog and doesn't even know it, and Obama is the cook who is doing it.

Why Socialism Fails Every Time

The dictionary defines *socialism* as: "a theory or system of social organization that advocates the vesting of the ownership and control of the means of production and distribution, of capital, land, etc., in the community as a whole." In other words, government owns or controls the means of production.

First, when government owns or controls the means of production, there is no longer any legitimate competition, only government control. The resulting inflationary prices then must be controlled by the government, which in turn creates shortages.

Secondly, entrepreneurs disappear, because who can compete with a government monopoly? Consequently, innovation, invention, and product development come to a screeching halt.

So far, the big banks, Wall Street, AIG, General Motors and Chrysler have fallen into the trap. Health-care is next.

In every case where socialism has been tried in the past, they found that in order to keep it from falling apart, they had to take away people's freedom, as in the USSR or Nazi Germany. The power was given to a totalitarian elite group of men and women.

There is no such thing as a free-market socialist state. They all became totalitarian, as renowned Austrian economist, F. A. Hayek, explained in his classic book, *The Road to Serfdom*.

All socialist states quickly learn they can't sustain themselves without a totalitarian elite controlling everyone. Eventually, every life is controlled down to the smallest detail. Call it Totalitarianism, Communism, Nazism or Fascism; these differ only in style, detail and structure, not in fact.

Galloping Socialism in America

Socialism is no longer creeping but galloping all around us. The White House and Congress are using the economic crisis to justify printing trillions of dollars in order to buy control of key industries with "bail-out" and alleged "stimulus" money. Due to this back-door nationalization of America, we (like other societies in the past) will quickly lose our freedom as government controls more and more of our lives.

The Obama Administration is totally committed to government-controlled socialism (is there any other kind?). The so-called "stimulus" was not for stimulus at all. It was just the smokescreen that provided the excuse for the funding which made a socialist agenda possible. Rahm Emanuel, Obama's Chief of Staff, spilled the beans when he publicly said, "You shouldn't waste a really good crisis!" He really meant that the financial crisis gave them a cover to do the things they always wanted to do politically.

Obama now controls all three branches of government. He reigns at the White House, has a liberal majority on the Supreme Court, and his party now controls the House of Representatives and the Senate with veto-proof majorities. He and his fellow leftists can now do literally anything they want.

Controlling the Media

The media (the fourth branch of government) loves Obama. With the media firmly in his pocket, Obama can do no wrong. He is the second coming of the Messiah. Liberals and Socialists control the movies, the news magazines, all three TV networks, the cable news networks, the big newspapers and music. Because the media is already overwhelmingly liberal, they don't just love Obama—they worship him. Watch one of his press conferences on TV and see just how much they adore him.

The free-market supporters in America that stand in opposition to Obama are pretty much limited to talk radio with

Rush Limbaugh, Sean Hannity, Glenn Beck, Mark Levin, and a few others. But for how long?

If you think those on the left are engaged in a civil debate of free ideas, think again. They intend to destroy the conservative right. Read a quote by Marcos Moulitsas, founder of the *Daily Kos* (probably the most widely read leftist/radical website):

> *"We have an imperative to take advantage of an historic opportunity to break conservative-movements' backs and crush their spirits. In the White House, that means getting Obama a broad geographic mandate for change. In the House, that means annihilating the Republican caucus and working toward a 100-seat Democratic majority in the Senate. It means getting to a 60-seat filibuster-proof majority."*

Recently, Obama has appointed FTC commissioners who, by the stroke of the regulatory pen, can make these conservative radio-talk shows untenable. How will this be done? Local orientation!

The FTC could simply rule that talk radio shows must "serve the community," which means everything will be locally orientated. Nationally syndicated talks shows will disappear because there is only so much airtime and stations will be required to feature hosts who will deal strictly with local (liberal) issues. It's a "community organizer's" dream.

Radio stations will lose all the attraction for advertisers that their big syndicated talk shows give them. This will be not only a terrible blow to the conservative talk show hosts but also a terrible blow to the stations. The strategy is really quite clever and easy to implement, and you can expect it sometime in the future. Some day the only place you will be able to hear anything about Obama may be from the media that already loves him.

An American Makeover: Obama's Real Agenda

No matter how he portrays himself, Obama has been a radical activist for most of his political career. He believes America needs an extreme makeover. That activism has been in support of organizations and initiatives that at their heart seek to tear the traditional pillars of this nation asunder in order to replace them with their demented socialist vision. For instance, he has pointed out certain "deficiencies" in the constitution that need to be fixed, namely that "it didn't mandate redistribution of income"— a purely socialist objective.

As stated before, Obama has had continuous, close relationships with radical, liberal extremists since college. It's not just guilt by *association* but guilt by *participation*.

Before his election to the US Senate, Obama spent time as a legislator in the blatantly corrupt machine that governs Illinois. Most telling, however, is his work with ACORN.

Once he got his law degree, he became an activist, starting with "neighborhood organizing." With the creation of ACORN (the Association of Community Organizations for Reform Now), he served as their lead counsel on many coercive, liberal programs while building a growing radical, socialist constituency.

What are ACORN and Obama Really Up To?

Following is excerpted from an article by James Simpson published in *The American Thinker*, September 28, 2008. What he reveals is alarming:

13

Obama has spent a large portion of his professional life working for ACORN or its subsidiaries, representing ACORN as a lawyer on some of its most critical issues, and training ACORN leaders. Stanley Kurtz's excellent National Review article, "Inside Obama's Acorn" also describes Obama's ACORN connection in detail. But I can't improve on Obama's own words:

"I've been fighting alongside ACORN on issues you care about my entire career (emphasis added). Even before I was an elected official, when I ran the Project Vote voter registration drive in Illinois, ACORN was smack dab in the middle of it, and we appreciate your work." —Barack Obama, Speech to ACORN, November 2007 (Courtesy Newsmax.)

As a community activist for ACORN; as a leadership trainer for ACORN; as a lead organizer for ACORN's Project Vote; as an attorney representing ACORN's successful efforts to impose Motor Voter regulations in Illinois; as ACORN's representative in lobbying for the expansion of high-risk housing loans through Fannie Mae and Freddie Mac that led to the current crisis; as a recipient of their assistance in his political campaigns—both with money and campaign workers; *it is doubtful that he was unaware of ACORN's true goals* [emphasis added].

In his few years (two) as a U.S. senator, Obama has received campaign contributions of $126,349 from Fannie Mac and Freddie Mac, second only to the $165,400 received by Senator Chris Dodd, who has been getting donations from them since 1988.

14

His closest advisers are a dirty laundry list of individuals at the heart of the financial crisis: former Fannie Mae CEO Jim Johnson; Former Fannie Mae CEO and former Clinton Budget Director Frank Raines; and billionaire failed Superior Bank of Chicago Board Chair Penny Pritzker.

Johnson had to step down as adviser on Obama's V.P. search after the following gem came out: An Office of Federal Housing Enterprise Oversight (OFHEO) report from September 2004 found that, during Johnson's tenure as CEO, Fannie Mae had improperly deferred $200 million in expenses, enabling top executives, including Johnson and his successor, Franklin Raines, to receive huge bonuses in 1998. A 2006 OFHEO report found that Fannie Mae had substantially under-reported Johnson's compensation. Johnson received approximately $21 million in bonuses.

Obama denies ties to Raines but the Washington Post calls him a member of "Obama's inner political circle." Raines and Johnson were fined $3 million by the Office of Federal Housing Oversight for their manipulation of Fannie books. The fine is small change however, compared to the $50 million Raines got in improper bonuses by juggling the books.

As a young attorney in the 1990s, Barack Obama represented ACORN in Washington in their successful efforts to make it easier for ACORN groups to force banks to make risky loans. This also paved the way for banks to package mortgages as investments, and for Government Sponsored

Enterprises Fannie Mae and Freddie Mac to underwrite them. *These changes created the conditions that ultimately led to the current financial crisis.*

Acorn's influence has spread so far and so wide that despite their blatant culpability in the current financial crisis due to Obama's influence, they are able to manipulate Capitol Hill politicians into cutting ACORN a $4 billion piece of the stimulus bailout pie!

Stimulus Lies

Working in cahoots with the Federal Reserve, Obama announced the government would spend almost a trillion dollars on a so-called "stimulus" program. I say "so-called" because this program was not designed to produce any economic stimulus. It was introduced to induce Congress to give the White House trillions of dollars with which to buy control of significant parts of the private sector.

Printing all these trillions of dollars (we don't actually print much money anymore; only about five percent is printed, minted or coined; the rest is created by a keystroke on a computer) only guarantees all this "stimulus" will only stimulate inflation and the growth of government.

First, spending money to stimulate a sick economy is discredited "Keynesian Economics." As the Japanese found out recently during their ten-year economic doldrums, "priming the pump" didn't work. It hasn't worked in the past, it won't work in the future, and it doesn't work now.

Second, most of the stimulus money was "back-loaded," which meant that only about five percent would be spent in 2009, and the rest would be spent years down the road. The current stimulus effect was near non-existent. Already the usual cast of characters is telling us the stimulus is not working because they underestimated the seriousness of the crisis, and the "stimulus" was "too small," so expect Stimulus Number Two!

The money they threw at the automobile industry had socialist strings attached. Basically, government bought control. They then fired the CEO of General Motors, and would not give the automobile industry the money unless they agreed to manufacture the kind of cars their environmentalist constituents wanted built, regardless of whether or not consumers wanted to buy them. The government and the unions ended up owning 89 percent of G.M. (Government Motors?), and "secured creditor" bondholders needing income were wiped out. So much for contracts. The American automobile industry was summarily "socialized."

The banks are under the thumb of government too. There were shotgun marriages such as when Bank of America had to buy Merrill Lynch with inadequate stockholder disclosure of Merrill's big problems. When billions were given to AIG, they were no longer permitted to reward the managers and successful sales people with the bonuses they had worked for and earned. Many employees had worked for "a dollar a year plus bonuses," but the government "cancelled" those rightful bonuses. How Obama expects AIG to ever make any money to repay taxpayers when their best people have been dis-incentivized and have run for cover, I'll never know.

Now you see how government is systematically, deliberately buying control of major industries. In fact, Barney Frank, one of the more powerful members of the Democratic caucus in the House, has been talking about controlling executive compensation even when the companies haven't taken any government money. In other words, the government plans to bully even private companies they have no financial claim on.

Yes, the Obama-induced advance of socialism will make things a lot worse in America (as it has in every other country on the globe), and if he gets his way, the government will control more and more of your life in an attempt to "fix" the problems it created.

Obama scares the wits out of me because he is destroying the fundamental economic freedom that has allowed this country to prosper for centuries. If he isn't the political anti-Christ, he'll do until one comes along.

The Good News Is...

Really, Obama has painted himself into a corner. If he thinks he has troubles now, wait until inflation really starts taking off and his plan is laid bare for the devastating mess he has created.

CHAPTER 2

How We Got In This Mess:
THE HISTORY OF THIS RECESSION,
INCLUDING WHO TO BLAME
(I NAME NAMES)

It is well enough that people of the nation do not understand
our banking and monetary system, for if they did, I believe there
would be a revolution before tomorrow morning.
—Henry Ford

The trends that led to the recent economic collapse have been festering for years. The basic root lies in one forever principle: half of Americans bought and paid for the Obamanation and are at the root of Obamanomics.

First, half of Americans don't pay a penny of taxes, so there is no constituency for cutting taxes. After all, everything is paid for by taxing those evil rich guys, right?

Second, half of all Americans receive a check from some level of government, so there is no constituency for cutting spending. The

19

average American doesn't pay for it, so why should they worry? They depend on their government checks such as student loans, federal and state employee paychecks, pension checks, Social Security, disability, Medicare, Medicaid, other entitlements, etc., etc., etc.

How We Got Here, Step by Step

Wall Street as we once knew it no longer exists, and is now a hiss and a byword, or at least a dead letter.

Merrill Lynch is joined in a shotgun merger with Bank of America. Washington Mutual, Fannie Mae and Freddie Mac are sick nigh unto death, and without government infusions they would be dead. Bear Stearns and Lehman Brothers are either bankrupt or merged. Citibank and AIG are near collapse and probably should fold. GM and Chrysler are now government owned and controlled. The government has taken control of almost everything we used to call Wall Street.

And in all this chaos, the economy is sick, unemployment is soaring, and government is growing like a weed. How did this all happen in the blink of an eye? Whose fault is it? How will all this change your life, even in small-town America? Most importantly, is there opportunity here?

I won't tell government what to do (they wouldn't listen to me anyway), but I will tell *you* what will really happen. My goal is to help middle-class Americans cope with the world as it really will be and even profit from it.

Buying Homes and Votes

It all started with a naked Democrat-driven political decision in Congress in the late 1970s. They realized they could acquire more votes if they helped people get a mortgage who previously couldn't qualify. These new candidates for home ownership (usually poor minorities) would likely return the favor by voting for Democrats (like Barney Frank, Christopher Dodd, and Teddy Kennedy).

So Congress, including many weak-kneed "moderate" Republicans (like Susan Collins, Arlen Specter, etc.), passed laws prohibiting banks from using a practice called "red lining"—writing off certain neighborhoods for disapproval of mortgages because most buyers who lived there were too poor to qualify financially or credit wise. Bankers assumed that "birds of a feather flock together," and the banks legitimately worried that loans might not ever be repaid.

Over the years, Congress passed additional criminal penalties for banks and mortgage companies that turned down a mortgage request for almost any reason, legitimate or not.

Thanks to government intervention, people who really could not afford mortgage payments, didn't have a down payment, or lacked good credit could now get a home mortgage and become "homeowners."

Additional pressure came from mobs of radical, left wing activists (ACORN?) who would sit outside the offices of CEOs of lending institutions and intimidate them into granting mortgages that should have been declined.

Cashing In

Bankers and mortgage lenders, seeing billions in potential business because of the millions of newly qualified homebuyers, then got into the act. Mortgage companies quickly saw they could earn big commissions by approving millions of new mortgages. They offered programs to entice these potential homebuyers: Adjustable-Rate Mortgages (ARMs) with low starting rates, after which the interest rate would jump up; "no-interest" loans; no-down-payment loans; or "no-document" loans without proof of income (behind closed doors they were called "liar's loans"). Stupid and ignorant homebuyers who either could not or did not read the small print in their contracts signed on the dotted line.

The National Real Estate Bubble

This mob of new homebuyers began to drive the growth of a huge real estate bubble. As residential real estate sales soared, so did prices due to increased demand. In addition, the Federal Reserve kept interest rates as low as one percent for years, making a mortgage even more "affordable".

Since buyers believed home prices would always go up, they assumed they could just refinance the homes at a higher price down the road if necessary. Because they had no skin in the game (no down payment, thus no equity), they had nothing to risk.

Then . . . surprise! Interest rates rose slightly and suddenly millions of homeowners found their mortgage payments had also risen, and they couldn't afford them. Foreclosures began to soar, first slowly, then faster, and home prices began to fall. As real estate prices topped out and foreclosures grew, the inventory of unsold properties started to rise, and sales and prices collapsed as the bubble deflated.

As the recession deepened and unemployment rose, soon millions couldn't make their mortgage payments and the rate of foreclosures gained momentum.

Homeowners could not refinance or sell their homes. Home values plummeted (and they still are dropping as this is written). People with no cash invested in their homes thought, "I can just walk away from it; I can't lose any equity, because I don't have any."

A wave of foreclosures swept across the country. Vacant, foreclosed homes drove down the value of *all* homes, even for those people who were current on their thirty-year, fixed-rate mortgages. Soon millions owed more than their homes were worth.

Mortgage Backed Securities

Now the plot thickens. When times were good, the bankers and mortgage brokers had bundled their mortgages into bond-like instruments called "Mortgage-Backed Securities" (MBS) and sold them to investors, banks, and big financial firms world-wide, thereby giving the brokers more cash to loan again to new buyers. MBSs became the foundation of the balance sheets of the world's largest financial institutions.

The credit-rating agencies gave these securities AAA ratings because they were "secured by real estate," so the world's largest banks and other financial institutions bought them for their portfolios in droves. AAA rated? Why not! MBSs were paying higher yields than almost anything else.

When it dawned on some that many of these mortgages might not be worth the paper they were written on and forecloses rose, the value of the underlying security, the real estate, began to be in question as rising real estate prices reversed. The financial institutions that had added MBSs to their balance sheets found to their horror they could not accurately determine the real market value of their portfolios.

GAAP

So how did giant Wall Street institutions like Merrill Lynch or Lehman Brothers fail so abruptly? GAAP (Generally Accepted Accounting Principles) accounting rules were modified by the Accounting Board so financial institutions had to "mark to market" the assets on their balance sheets. If the market had no bid nor ask, no one knew what the MBSs were really worth. With no market quotes, the market for MBSs dried up.

When billions of assets on their balance sheets could not be valued (marked to a non-existent market), the banks' accountants often gave many of them zero value. Overnight, when large portions of their balance sheets had disappeared, the banks didn't have enough assets to meet the statutory requirements for cash reserves.

To complicate the situation further, banks could not loan or borrow from each other, because most of them were in the same boat. When a bank or brokerage house's balance sheet is deeply impaired, they have to raise additional capital. When that's happening to everyone, who will loan the money?

Wall Street Implosion

Almost overnight, big institutions that had invested heavily in these mortgage-backed securities began to fail. That's when Wall Street imploded. Goodbye Merrill Lynch, Lehman Brothers, Washington Mutual, Bear Stearns, etc.

I previously wrote in *The Ruff Times*: "The issuance of mortgage-backed securities began to decline with less money inflow into the system, and home prices began to fall faster, throwing the whole bubble into reverse. Since the viability of the related paper assets was dependent upon rising real estate prices and asset valuations, the entire edifice began to crumble."

The turmoil at Bear Stearns is illustrative. Bear Stearns had made lots of money speculating in sub-prime real estate by buying sub-prime loans (no documentation of earnings or no down payment) and selling and buying MBSs.

Though the amount of money involved in the Bear Stearns crisis was relatively small, the implications of the phony and suspect MBS values sent shock waves reverberating through a system chockfull of such phony valuations. Trillions upon trillions of dollars of bank assets were based on low valuations, unrecoverable debt, and no proven market value.

Reduced flow into the financial system and the vaporization of bank asset values created the "credit crunch" which is causing all the panic. Businessmen found that the loan capital they were counting on had dried up. Giant Lehman Brothers folded and went bankrupt. Hedge funds began to fail left and right, others took heavy paper losses, and still others forbade nervous investors from withdrawing their money. The very system itself was vaporizing, because the value of the assets on their balance sheets was suspect, to say the least.

The entire global financial system suffered because big financial institutions all over the world had invested in MBSs and added them to their balance sheets. Consolidations have disguised many failures by the movement of bad assets off their books via the derivatives markets and phony accounting—with the complicity of regulators and guilty politicians worldwide. Some big banks are bankrupt several times over, protected only by the *illusion* that the assets on their books have value, but those illusions (which are all that kept the banks open) have faded.

Global Panic

As the level of the panic rose around the world, the Fed turned on the money spigots, realizing the scope of the losses facing the entire system. Congress panicked, the White House panicked, the markets panicked, the banks panicked, and the Fed panicked. Irrational fear started calling all the financial shots, and the game was over.

The end result was that the White House, under the guise of "stimulus," used almost $1 trillion (created out of nothing) to bail out and control Wall Street. The money was allegedly to be used to buy up the bad mortgages from banks and alter the contract terms to stop foreclosures so millions, no matter how unworthy, could own a house they couldn't lose—whether they made the mortgage payments or not.

The MBS Meltdown Parable

One of my subscribers sent me the following parable. I've seen it posted on several websites. It's instructional—and amusing.

Heidi is the proprietor of a bar in Detroit. Virtually all of her customers are unemployed alcoholics and can no longer afford to patronize her bar. To solve this problem, she comes up with a new marketing plan that allows her customers to drink now, but pay later. On the ledger, she keeps track of the drinks consumed, granting the customers loans.

Soon she has the largest sales volume of any bar in Detroit.

Heidi gets no resistance when she substantially increases her prices for wine and beer. Heidi's gross sales volume increases massively.

A vice-president at the local bank recognizes that these customer debts constitute valuable future assets and increases Heidi's borrowing limit. He sees no reason for any undue concern, since he has the debts of the unemployed alcoholics as collateral.

The bank transforms these customer loans into DRINK-BONDS, ALKIBONDS and PUKEBONDS. These securities are then bundled and traded on the international security markets. Naive investors didn't really understand that the securities being sold to them as AAA secured bonds are really the debts of unemployed alcoholics.

Bond prices continuously climb, and the securities become the hottest-selling items for some of the nation's leading brokerage houses.

One day a risk manager at the original bank decides that the time has come to demand payment on the debts. He informs Heidi.

Heidi then demands payment from her alcoholic patrons, but being unemployed alcoholics they cannot pay their drinking debts. Since Heidi cannot fulfill her loan obligations she is forced into bankruptcy. The bar closes and eleven employees lose their jobs.

Overnight, DRINKBONDS, ALKIBONDS and PUKE-BONDS drop in price by 90%. The collapsed bond-asset value destroys the bank's liquidity and prevents it from issuing new loans, thus freezing credit and economic activity in the community.

The suppliers of Heidi's bar had granted her generous payment extensions and had invested their firms' pension funds in the various BOND securities. They find they now must write off her bad debt, losing over 90% of the presumed value of the bonds. Her wine supplier also claims bankruptcy, closing the doors on a family business that had endured for three generations. Her beer supplier is taken over by a competitor, who immediately closes the local plant and lays off 150 workers.

Fortunately though, the bank, the brokerage houses and their respective executives are bailed out by a multi-billion dollar no-strings-attached cash infusion from the government. The funds are obtained by new taxes levied on the employed middle-class, and non-drinkers.

Now do you understand?

The Root of the Problem

Congress and the Administration played lifeguard and bailed out these firms that were hit by the mortgage crisis. But government money is not without its strings. The government took huge equity positions as part of the price of their loans and took legal control of what was left of Wall Street.

At the same time, Obama made more than a trillion dollars (understated) in additional new promises to buy votes for the sake of "stimulus." He subcontracted the job to Harry Reid and Nancy Pelosi. They sent Congress the 1100-page stimulus document at 10:00 p.m. the night before the vote, and it passed almost unanimously, *AND NO ONE HAD READ THE DOCUMENT BEFORE THE VOTE.* It was mostly a 40-year wish list of leftist priorities.

At the End of the Day

To sum up, this economic mess had five roots: **1)** a political decision in Congress to buy votes; **2)** the unprecedented view that everyone should own a home, whether they could afford it or not; **3)** the tightening of bankers' and mortgage brokers' accounting rules; **4)** ignorant and unsophisticated homebuyers didn't or couldn't read the small print in their contracts; and **5)** greedy bankers and mortgage company CEOs jumped on the real estate gravy train.

This is not just the Democrats' fault; most Republicans forgot their alleged conservative principles and became enablers. George W. Bush, for instance, gave billions to GM.

Ironically, guess who was asked to fix the mess? The very ones who caused the initial problem in the first place! Barney Frank and Chris Dodd were star performers in the meltdown, along with Jim Johnson and Frank Raines, former CEOs of Fannie Mae who took huge bonuses by misrepresenting Fannie May's profits. These men are now in Obama's inner circle.

If Washington really wanted to find the villains, they should have looked in the mirror. Unfortunately, the average American has no grasp of the real facts, so they are easily buffaloed.

This huge problem is almost beyond the ingenuity of human leadership; it is so big and perverse that Congress is spending trillions of dollars to fix it, but even that's not working. So far it is estimated that seventy-five percent of the alleged loan modifications will default again in six months to a year, even though payments were lowered to thirty-one percent of their income. We haven't seen the last of the problem.

CHAPTER 3

Offspring–I Never Knew You:
THE FALLOUT OF ENTITLEMENTS
AND YOUTHFUL INGRATITUDE

Material abundance without character is the path of destruction.
—Thomas Jefferson

For several decades America has worshiped at the altar of youth. Old timers like me who have been through ups and downs over the decades are simply ignored or laughed at. We are the first dominant society that did not respect its elders as sources of wisdom and judgment.

Take, for instance, the 1960s Cultural Revolution. This movement changed America forever. It turned America against the Vietnam War and created the professors that became leftist department heads at the universities. Unbelievably, the whole thing was based on the absurd assumption that college-age kids are not just smart, but wise.

No, they are not! I may be biased because I am one of the old guys, but the ignorance and inexperience of young people across

America is often appalling. They have never known anything but being supported by their parents, by student loans, by credit cards, and by government checks. Unlike my generation, they don't know how to labor or go without.

They won't lead us to a bright new future. They can't! They have neither the character nor the knowledge.

These naïve kids massively voted for Barack Obama, and look what they got—a socialist, as in their youthful exuberance, they perceived him as a charismatic, charming and attractive. They don't understand his policies or their ramifications; they just like how he looks and how he sounds.

Our kids are being brainwashed at every major university in America, creating more leftist graduates who teach our impressionable children in our public schools. Our teacher-college faculties are overwhelmingly liberal and have bought into the socialist dogma. This is one reason why leftism is an irresistible force.

The following is from an Op Ed piece in *The Wall Street Journal* written by Stephen Moore on June 19, 2009 (reprinted with permission). Mr. Moore is a senior-economics writer for *The Wall Street Journal's* editorial page. He writes:

> *Last weekend I attended my niece's high-school graduation from an upscale prep school in Washington, D.C. These events are supposed to be filled with joy, optimism and anticipation of great achievements. But nearly all the kids dutifully moaned about how terrified they are of America's future—yes, even though Barack Obama, whom they all worship and adore, has brought "change they can believe in." A federal*

judge gave the commencement address and denounced the sorry state of the nation that will be handed off to them. The enemy, he said, is the collective narcissism of their parents' generation—my generation. The judge said that we baby boomers have bequeathed to them a legacy of "greed, global warming, and growing income inequality."

And every one of all age groups seemed to agree. One affluent 40-something woman with lots of jewelry told me she can barely look her teenagers in the eyes, so overcome is she with shame over the miseries we have bestowed upon our children.

Graduation ceremonies have become collective airings of guilt and grief! It's now chic for boomers to apologize for their generation's crimes. Conservatives and liberals seem to agree. Mitch Daniels, the Republican governor of Indiana, told Butler University grads that our generation is "just plain selfish." Filmmaker Ken Burns told Boston College grads that those born between 1946 and 1960 have 'squandered the legacy handed to them by the World War II generation.'

"We partied like it was 1999, paid for it with Ponzi schemes and left the mess for our kids and grandkids to clean up. We're sorry—so sorry."

I'm not! I have two teenagers and an eight-year-old, and can say firsthand that if boomer parents have anything for which to be sorry, it's for rearing a generation of pampered kids who've been chauffeured around to soccer leagues since they were six. This is a generation that regards rising affluence as a basic human right, because that is all it has ever known—until now. Today's high school and college *students think iPods, designer cell phones, and $599 laptops are entitlements*

CBS News reported recently that echo boomers spend $170 billion a year— more than most nations' GDPs—and nearly every penny of that comes from the wallets of the very parents they now resent. My parents' generation lived in fear of polio, and many boomers lived in fear of going to Vietnam; this generation's notion of hardship is TiVo breaking down.

How bad can the legacy really be? Let's see: We're the generation that spawned Microsoft, Intel, Apple, Google, ATMs *and* Gatorade. *We defeated communism and delivered the world from the brink of global thermonuclear war. Now youngsters are telling pollsters that they think socialism may be better than capitalism after all. Do they next expect us to apologize for winning the Cold War?*

College students gripe about the price of tuition, and it does cost way too much. But who do these 22-year-old scholars think has been footing the bill for their courses in Transgender Studies and Che Guevara? The echo boomers complain that we have left them holding the government's $8 trillion national IOU. Try to cut government aid to colleges or raise tuitions and they act like they have been forced to actually work for a living.

So how about a little gratitude from these trust-fund babies?

My generation is accused of being "environmental crimi-nals" —of having polluted the water and air and ruined the climate. No generation in history has done more to clean the environment than mine. Since 1970, pollutants in the air and water have fallen sharply. Since 1960, many cities have cut in half the number of days with unsafe levels of smog. The number of Americans who get sick or die from contaminants in our drinking water has plunged for 50 years straight.

Whenever kids ask me why we didn't do more to combat global warming, I explain that when I was young, the "scientific consensus" warned of global cooling. Today's teenagers drive around in cars more than any previous generation. My kids have never once handed back the car keys because of some moral problem with their carbon footprint.

The most absurd complaint of all is that the healthcare system has been ruined by our generation. Oh, really? Thanks to massive medical progress in the past 30 years, the chances of dying from heart disease and many types of cancer have been cut in half. We found effective treatments for AIDS within a decade. Life expectancy has risen and infant mortality fallen. That doesn't sound so "selfish" to me.

Yes, we are in a deep economic crisis today—but it's no worse than what we boomers faced in the late 1970s after years of hyperinflation, sky-high tax rates and runaway government spending. We cursed our parents, too. But then we grew up and produced a big leap forward in health, wealth and scientific progress. Let's see what this next generation of over-educated ingrates can do.

I can't say it any better than Mr. Moore. Thank goodness most of my offspring don't fit this graphic description!

CHAPTER 4

The Assault on the Traditional Family:
THE COST OF SEXUAL ANARCHY

Our Constitution was made only for a religious and moral people.
It is wholly inadequate for the government of any other.
—John Adams

This may be the most important chapter of this book. The most dangerous direction of the Obamanation, with the worst consequences for America, is the calculated assault on the traditional family. It's very apparent that those with radical sexual views have a friend in the Whitehouse.

This attack is spearheaded by what I call *sexual anarchists*—the radical abortionists, the radical homosexuals, the LGBT "community" (Lesbian, Gay, Bi-sexual, and Transgender; Sounds like a sandwich, doesn't it? BLT, anyone?), and all those who want their irresponsible or perverted sexual orientation to become an accepted worldwide standard.

Though a small minority, LGBT individuals are important to politicians who are looking to buy votes. The LGBT community tends to be more affluent and liquid than the rest of us. Because they are free of the expensive burden of children and family responsibilities, they can contribute huge sums of money to the political party that caters to them and is willing to normalize their behavior.

They also tend to be relentlessly vocal and even militant as they push their agenda, especially when they encounter opposition.

Traditional American Values

Just to be honest with you, I believe these "anarchisms" are the very definition of "adultery and fornication" in all their varieties. Every Christian or Muslim (and that's a large percentage of the world population) believes any sex outside standard marriage between a man and a woman is a sin, including homosexuality, incest, cohabitation and pre-marital sex. They are just different sides of the same coin.

But God has given us free will. It's not my job to punish sinners or prevent individual sin. God has not given me that authority. I am not bashing homosexuality or other sexual "orientations" by consenting adults. Although I may not agree with this tiny minority, their personal sexual habits are none of my business.

I only oppose the radical political agenda that seeks to make sexual perversions legally and philosophically acceptable; I oppose the attempt to set homosexuality up as the routine equivalent of male/female sexual marital relations; and I oppose attempts to make abortion on demand the American standard. It horrifies me that the most helpless human lives are being snuffed out before they have even seen the light of day.

The Same-sex Marriage Wedge

Homosexual marriage is a wedge issue. If homosexual marriage is made legal, the sexual anarchists will have established a precedent to legalizing incest, pedophilia, and virtually every other unholy kind of relationship. Pornography and sexual confusion will be the order of the day.

Once homosexual marriage is legal, schools must teach our children that this is morally and legally equivalent to heterosexual marriage. It follows that any kind of sexual activity is acceptable, including pre-marital adolescent sex. What can a Christian or Muslim family do when they are trying to teach traditional standards to their children at home and church or mosque, and they are being taught something different at school?

Friends have told me they don't really care if homosexuals can get married because "it doesn't affect my life or marriage" . . . but it does! Its impact *will* be felt by your children and grandchildren, and perhaps the most devastating impact is still two or three generations away.

As human beings, we may be free to choose our behavior, but we can't choose our consequences. The result of this promotion of sexual anarchy will be adolescent sexual activity, out-of-wedlock pregnancies with teenagers unequipped financially and emotionally to handle the responsibility of a child, and millions turning to abortion to make reality go away. Sexual anarchy tears apart the family unit and creates broken families.

Lessons from Proposition 8

On a personal note, I got a real taste of the basic LGBT strategy during the battle over Proposition 8 in California. One of my children and her family at the urging of LDS (Mormon) Church Leaders decided to contribute half their savings, a considerable sum, to the campaign to win Proposition 8, which opposed homosexual marriage. The *Sacramento Bee* did a front-page story on them, complete with pictures. I carefully read all the comments that were emailed to the *Sacramento Bee* and the one repeated theme was that we Mormons must be motivated by "hate and bigotry." One comment said, "They must have learned this from their parents." That's Kay and me.

It's ironic that those who scream the loudest for tolerance are often the most intolerant among us! My children and grandchildren don't have a bigoted bone in their bodies. I have hired known homosexuals to work for me in positions of responsibility; they were qualified to do the job and were discreet in their behavior. Their private sexual behavior, however distasteful to me, was none of my business.

But it *is* my business to stand up against what I feel is wrong.

As I responded to those comments by email, I told them I did **not** teach hate to my children. If they practice hate or bigotry, they are not practicing their religion. I stated that there are lots of legitimate moral and philosophical reasons to oppose Prop 8, none of which were motivated by hate or bigotry.

The UN in the Spotlight

For decades, the sexual anarchists worldwide have been concentrating their firepower on the United Nations. Radical NGOs

(Non-Governmental Organizations) participate in and often control the agenda at UN conferences around the world. These organizations deliberately form and promote UN resolutions that impose the sexual attitudes of the radical, well-organized, well-financed minority upon the world as a whole. They know that if they can pass resolutions at the UN, those resolutions will become part of "customary international law."

Because international law sets a precedent, what happens at the UN has more and more influence on what happens at home. American judges, even on the Supreme Court, are now sometimes ignoring the Constitution and citing foreign law in support of their decisions, and it's happening with increasing frequency.

Inroads into Public Education

The sexual anarchists are not just manipulating the UN but are making great inroads into the hearts and minds of our children through our public schools. Children are too often being taught that to criticize homosexuality or abortion on religious grounds is "hate speech" and should be punished.

Adolescents often have periods of sexual confusion, but the sexual activists and lobbyists are telling them that it is as good to be sexually active or homosexual as it is to be a married heterosexual. The sexual anarchists are deliberately trying to condition and confuse our young people during the vulnerable time while they are trying to figure out their sexual identity.

How Obama Cheers on the Sexual Radicals

Sexual anarchists are trying to create a world where any kind of sexual relationship is okay, and Obama is giving legitimacy to their anarchistic behavior. The apparent traditional family values portrayed by the Obama family in the White House just seems like camouflage. From his actions, it appears Obama wants to turn America into a country that is tolerant of any and all sexual deviations.

Obama's Proclamation

In June of 2009, the Obama administration posted the following proclamation on the White House web site:

LESBIAN, GAY, BISEXUAL, AND TRANSGENDER PRIDE MONTH, 2009

BY THE PRESIDENT OF THE UNITED STATES OF AMERICA, A PROCLAMATION

Forty years ago, patrons and supporters of the Stonewall Inn in New York City resisted police harassment that had become all too common for members of the lesbian, gay, bisexual, and transgender (LGBT) community. Out of this resistance, the LGBT rights movement in America was born. During LGBT Pride Month, we commemorate the events of June 1969 and commit to achieving equal justice under law for LGBT Americans.

LGBT Americans have made, and continue to make, great and lasting contributions that continue to strengthen the fabric of American society. There are many well-respected LGBT leaders in all professional fields, including the arts and business communities. LGBT Americans also mobilized the Nation to respond to the domestic HIV/AIDS epidemic and have played a vital role in broadening this country's response to the HIV pandemic. (They are spreading HIV with their promiscuous behavior. HJR)

Due in no small part to the determination and dedication of the LGBT rights movement; more LGBT Americans are living their lives openly today than ever before. I am proud to be the first President to appoint openly LGBT candidates to Senate-confirmed positions in the first 100 days of an Administration. These individuals embody the best qualities we seek in public servants, and across my Administration — in both the White House and the Federal agencies — openly LGBT employees are doing their jobs with distinction and professionalism.

The LGBT rights movement has achieved great progress, but there is more work to be done. LGBT youth should feel safe to learn without the fear of harassment, and LGBT families and seniors should be allowed to live their lives with dignity and respect.

My Administration has partnered with the LGBT community to advance a wide range of initiatives. At the international level, I have joined efforts at the United Nations to decriminalize homosexuality around the world. Here at home, I continue to support measures to bring the full spectrum of equal rights to LGBT Americans. These measures include enhancing hate-crimes laws, supporting civil unions and Federal rights for LGBT couples, outlawing discrimination in the workplace, ensuring adoption rights, and ending the existing "Don't Ask, Don't Tell" policy in a way that strengthens our Armed Forces and our national security. We must also commit ourselves to fighting the HIV/AIDS epidemic by both reducing the number of HIV infections and providing care and support services to people living with HIV/AIDS across the United States.

These issues affect not only the LGBT community, but also our entire Nation. As long as the promise of equality for all remains unfulfilled, all Americans are affected. If we can work together to advance the principles upon which our Nation was founded, every American will benefit. During LGBT Pride Month, I call upon the LGBT community, the Congress, and the American people to work together to promote equal rights for all, regardless of sexual orientation or gender identity.

NOW, THEREFORE, I, BARACK OBAMA, President of the United States of America, by virtue of the authority vested in me by the Constitution and laws of the United States do hereby proclaim June 2009 as Lesbian, Gay, Bisexual, and Transgender Pride Month. I call upon the people of the United States to turn back discrimination and prejudice everywhere it exists.

BARACK OBAMA

With this proclamation, the president of the United States has established himself as a leader in the movement to promote homosexuality, abortion and transgenderism, not just in the United States but across the world as well. No wonder some of the extreme Islamic fundamentalists want to bomb "The Great Satan."

When Barack Obama issued that proclamation, I didn't see it in any newspaper, including *The Wall Street Journal*. It may be the most subversive thing he has ever done—all to buy the votes of a tiny two percent minority.

The Obama Administration at the UN

At a recent UN conference, my daughter, *Sharon Slater*, President of *Family Watch International*, met with a woman who represented Obama's administration. Sharon was there to fight against the endorsement of a document calling not only for worldwide legalization of same-sex marriage, abortion, and prostitution but also for penalties against anyone who criticizes homosexuality, among other things.

When Sharon asked the US delegate if the Obama administration would be willing to oppose the resolution (since President Obama stated as a candidate he was against legalizing same sex marriage), the delegate told Sharon, "My instructions are to support these resolutions."

Obama and Kevin Jennings

Obama's inner-circle is shaping-up like the bar scene from Star Wars. It's a swollen throng of unaccountable czars and policy advisors comprised of some of the most bizarre fringe leftists imaginable. As mom always said, you're known by the company you keep and Obama keeps some downright creepy company.

Perhaps the creepiest of Obama's advisers is "safe schools" chief Kevin Jennings. Jennings—an open homosexual activist—is former director of GLSEN (the Gay, Lesbian and Straight Education Network), a group of adult homosexual activists who promote sexual anarchy and tacitly work to normalize the criminal practice of pederasty.

He even penned the foreword to a book entitled "Queering Elementary Education."

Jennings' organization sponsored pornographic material at Brookline High School in Massachusetts in 2005. He taught a session to schoolchildren on how to engage in homosexual acts.

Stand Firm

We, the traditional and moral majority, can and must vigorously resist the attempts of the sexual radicals to impose their agenda on us and our children by using the law and our public schools (not to mention the entertainment industry) to legitimatize themselves.

My resistance is not aimed at individual behavior or "sin." It has nothing to do with the personal morals of consenting adults. I'm not interested in peering into their bedrooms or gay bars. I simply don't want to allow perverse relationships to become the legal and functional equivalent of the traditional marriage that has held America together for many decades.

So, I actively resist these breath-taking changes in society, as do many of my family members. I previously mentioned my daughter, Sharon Slater, president of Family Watch International. I fully support Sharon's work and have contributed money to support her. I ask you to do the same.

To donate and/or receive free weekly updates on issues that impact families worldwide, you can sign up for her free online newsletter, *The Family Watch*. Go to www.familywatchinternational.org. You can also mail a donation to:

Family Watch International
PO Box 1432
Gilbert, AZ 85299-1432
Phone: 480-507-2664

Sharon has also written a new book, *Stand for the Family*, which exposes the overt and covert threats to the family (I have only scratched the surface of these vicious attacks here) and tells you what you can do about them. To order the book (all proceeds go to support efforts to defend the traditional family) go to www.standforthefamily.org, or call the number above.

PART II

ON THE HORIZON: THE ECONOMIC STORM OF THE CENTURY

CHAPTER 5

The Phony Socialist Health-Care Crisis:
THE BIGGEST POWER-GRAB OF ALL

A government that is big enough to give you all you want
is big enough to take it all away.
—Barry Goldwater

We are inevitably following the rest of the world into the fetid swamps of a massive national health-care (sick care?) program. It will dwarf all current expenditures on Social Security, Medicare, and Medicaid by trillions of dollars—and they are already burying us! It's the ultimate socialist grab for power.

The average politically ignorant American who ignores or knows nothing about history will say, "Why not? Other countries do it? Why not us?"

Why not? For the simple reason that it doesn't work in other countries and it won't work here.

The consequence of national health-care will be rationing. When we discover we can't afford to do everything that was promised, we will have to ration it by price and time. The only way for Obama to keep his promises about the lower cost of health-care is by price controls, which will make it cheaper, yes, but you'll have to wait in line for service, often for months. Seniors will be denied care that costs too much, like chemotherapy or heart-bypass surgery.

All the health-care promises that are being made are impossible to keep. Some government agency will determine whether or not it is cost effective to use an expensive new drug or procedure that might cure you, but if in their cold-blooded opinion it costs too much because you are too old, *you will not be allowed to buy it personally at any price*. Bureaucrats alone, not doctors, will make those life-and-death decisions.

Soon your family doctor will give up the health-care business because he can't cope with all the government forms, he'll be swamped by trying to help too many patients, and the government keeps underpaying him. He will have to work harder for less money, so who could blame him for quitting?

The doctor shortage will only get worse when fewer and fewer students are willing to become doctors because it's not worth the return on investment medical school requires.

Sick Care

Honestly, we're not really talking about health-care; we're talking about "sick care," even in America. Our system isn't designed to keep you healthy; even our current system only helps you if you get sick or injured.

It's like laws against guns. People buy guns to protect themselves because the police will only help you if a crime has already been committed. Law enforcement will do little or nothing to help prevent the crime.

It's the same thing with your doctor. How many of you have ever gone to your doctor for a serious health checkup—to find out if you have a problem that could be treated in its early stages? Some of us do, but most don't. Maybe that's because health insurance has trouble paying for it.

Lessons from Canada

A U.S. national health-care program will mimic Canada's, where patients needing urgent treatment or surgery often have to wait for months—or they go to America, if they can afford it.

In Canada and several European countries, it is against the law to get around the national health-care system by paying a private practitioner. You have no choice, unless you are rich enough to go to America.

Dennis Gartman makes the following points in his newsletter, www.thegartmanletter.com. He says:

If you think government-controlled health-care is a good idea, consider this:

- *In the U.S. 93 percent of those diagnosed with diabetes receive treatment within six months. In Canada, only 43 percent do!*

- *For those seniors needing hip and knee replacement, 43 percent of Canadians get it done in six months ... in the U.S., 90 percent do*

- *In the U.S. there are 71 MRI or CT scanners available per every million people. In Canada, there are but 18.*

Heaven help you if you have something really wrong in Canada. If that's the case, you'll run south of the border faster than you can reach a specialist anywhere there.

I don't want some nameless bureaucrat deciding who gets to live or die in the name of his scientific and federal orthodoxy. Obama and the majority in Congress are planning bureaucrat rationing for our future, and senior citizens will suffer the most, and Obama is lying about it. As a senior, I have a target on my back.

Obama's Assault on Seniors

As this is written, legislation now being rammed through the House and Senate will pressure the elderly to end their life prematurely and doom baby-boomers to painful later years.

Democrats in Congress want to pay for the $1.6 trillion health bill with new taxes and a $500-billion cut to Medicare. The Congressional budget office estimates only one percent of Medicare cuts will come from "reform" aimed at eliminating fraud, waste, and abuse. That means the other 99 percent has to come from cutting benefits.

Comparative Effectiveness Research

The assault against seniors began with the stimulus package that became law in February, 2009. Slipped into the bill was substantial funding for "Comparative Effectiveness" research, which means "limiting care based on the patient's age." The cost of treatment (about $50,000 a year) is divided by the number of years that the patient is likely to benefit. In Britain, the formula leads to denying life-extending treatment for elderly patients who have fewer years to benefit from care than younger patients.

When Comparative Effectiveness appeared in the stimulus bill, Representative Charles Boustany, Jr. (R:LA), a heart surgeon, warned that it would lead to "denying seniors with expensive illnesses any life-giving care." He and Senator John Kyl (R:AZ) proposed to no avail amendments which would have barred the federal government from using the research to eliminate treatments for the elderly or to deny care based on age.

Nancy Pelosi and White House Budget Chief, Peter Orszag, asked Congress to delegate its authority over Medicare to a newly created body within the executive branch. This was obviously designed to circumvent the democratic process and avoid accountability to the public for cuts in benefits.

Medicare Cutbacks

Medicare is running out of money. The problem is there are too many seniors compared with the smaller number of workers supporting the system with payroll taxes. Inevitably, less money and more patients will necessitate rationing.

The Congressional Budget Office wants to inch up the eligibility age one month per year until it reaches age 70 in 2043. Wealthy seniors may also be required to pay more.

Until now, Medicare has made living to a ripe old age a good value. ObamaCare will undo that. Already, in Oregon, the state denies some elderly cancer patients care that would extend their lives. Instead, the state pays for "physician-assisted-suicide counseling."

The House bill being pushed by the President ensures seniors are given end-of-life options, including refusing them care when state law allows it. On page 425 of the Health-care Bill under consideration by the House of Representatives, it says in black and white that everyone on Social Security (which includes all senior citizens and Social Security recipients) will go to *mandatory* counseling every five years to learn (among other things) about how to choose a way to end your suffering and your life.

The Inescapable Truth

Americans need to see past the Washington lies. Health-care reform leads to only one place—bigger government, higher taxes, and health-care rationing. The facts are: the only way to slash $500 billion from Medicare is to drastically cut health-care for seniors; care will be denied based on age; the oldest and sickest will be cut first; and paying for your own care, if you can afford it, will not even be an option.

If you are over 65, be afraid.
Be very afraid!
If you think health-care is expensive now, wait until it's free.

CHAPTER 6

Inflation:
WHY HYPERINFLATION IS IN YOUR FUTURE

We are in danger of being overwhelmed with irredeemable paper,
mere paper, representing not gold nor silver; no sir, representing
nothing but broken promises, bad faith, bankrupt corporations,
cheated creditors and a ruined people.
—Daniel Webster

As the book is written, we are deep in a deflationary recession, which means prices are falling as a natural consequence of the falling economy. Deflation and inflation are monetary phenomena caused by creating more or less currency and shrinking or accelerating the velocity of money.

Money in Motion

A dollar created by the Federal Reserve that just sits there on the balance sheet of a bank is not inflationary, and government has given trillions of bailout dollars to banks. The banks have mostly just been sitting on the money to rehabilitate their balance sheets, but bankers will soon figure out that they can only make money by lending money, so they will loan it into circulation.

As the hoarded dollars eventually start moving through the economy, they will have the same effect as if more money were printed. Consequently, the root of a big-time hyperinflation is being planted as the government tries to fight deflation by throwing money at it.

Washington is now printing massive amounts of currency, based on the discredited Keynesian notion that you can borrow and spend your way out of an economic downturn. You can't! America has tried this before; it failed. Remember, Japan tried it for almost 20 years; it failed. The roots of the hyperinflation to come have been laid during this current deflation, because the government considers deflation and depression to be anonymous. Since no one in political power wants to be blamed for an economic downturn, they are printing massive amounts of money to "stimulate" the economy.

The side benefit for the politicians is that they can give money to their favorite constituencies and buy their votes. The end result will be a monster monetary hyperinflation, followed by soaring price inflation. We will experience levels of price inflation that have not been seen in America since it was founded.

What You Need to Know About Inflation

Inflation always disrupts the economy. You may make more money if your job has an "escalator clause," but that money will buy less and less. The price of gas and oil will go up and up, not because it's worth more or because there is a shortage of it, but because the price reflects the decreasing value of the unit of account—the dollar.

Inflation is good news and bad news. It's bad news for those who can't keep their income up with it, but it's good news for those who learn how to invest in it. Wise investors can actually turn small amounts of money into fortunes. Again, Will Rogers said it best: "Invest in inflation, it's the only thing that's going up."

Here are some fundamental things you need to know about inflation:

Too much paper money equals inflation. At all times and in all places ever since the creating of printing presses, inflation is caused by producing too much paper money. That's what we are now doing with trillions of dollars.

The velocity of money matters. The money has to be put into circulation. If the dollar circulates through the economy four times, it is four times as inflationary as a dollar that doesn't circulate. In fact, if the dollar just sits there and goes nowhere, it's not inflationary.

So far, when the trillions of dollars were given to the banks, they just used them to repair their balance sheets and deposited them at the Federal Reserve to earn interest. Because they have not gone into circulation, it has not yet created inflation, but it will.

The loss of the dollar prestige as it sags on the international markets in comparison to other currencies is a major cause and effect of inflation.

Dollar printing is triggered by people voting themselves benefits from government and by politicians using dollars to buy votes. It always ends up producing inflation and eventually destroys the currency.

Socialism always produces inflation. Socialist entitlement programs like Social Security, Medicare, Medicaid, and compulsory health-care will cause inflation simply because the Federal Reserve has to accommodate government promises by printing money. Nations get seduced into socialism by government promises of security because people want to get their check from government. Because people don't know the real cause of inflation, they fall for the scam and the entitlements pouring down from government become irreversible.

Eventually all socialist societies inflate their currency and the only way they know to fight inflation is by wage and price controls. However, when the government controls the price of goods below their production cost, people stop producing. That creates shortages. So, the government may make nominal attempts at "fighting inflation" but at the cost of shortages and rationing.

I remember being in Leningrad as our tour bus was stalled, watching hundreds of women running to a store to get in a line for something. They didn't even know what it was. They just knew something was for sale, so they wanted it. If they didn't want it themselves or couldn't use it, they could sell or barter it.

Socialism usually happens gradually, as the people naively believe that government will take care of them. It has been creeping in America for almost a hundred years, with the greatest impetus during the Roosevelt years.

The Socialist Party in America

Norman Thomas ran six times for the presidency as the candidate for the Socialist Party. He only won a few votes, mostly because "socialist" was a bad word back then. Some years later, after he was no longer the Socialist candidate for the Presidency, he was asked why he didn't run again. His answer? "The Socialist Party platform has been adopted by the Democratic Party, so there is no need for me to run."

When I checked with snopes.com, which debunks Internet myths, they could find no documentary proof Thomas made this statement. However, I received an email from Roger Clites, a subscriber to *The Ruff Times*, who taught economics at a small midwestern Christian college.

When he was a student, he attended a lecture by Norman Thomas. Mr. Thomas told the group, "The Democrats have put into place plank after plank of the socialist platform, and soon the Republicans will compete with them in an attempt to gain support from voters who don't understand what they are doing."

Almost everything on that platform, including Medicare, Welfare, Social Security, and all other benefits Americans receive from government were in that Socialist platform.

The Social Security Scam

As this is written, Social Security, Medicare, and Medicaid account for more than $40 trillion in unfunded liabilities (obligations supported by no income or assets) that can only be paid by inflating the currency (printing money).

Tens of millions of people don't question that Social Security will be there for them upon retirement and will provide a comfortable life. Even financial planners build this assumption into their financial plans.

Truthfully, for millions of Americans, this is a lie. It will be an expensive and painful mistake to bet on Social Security.

Many of you already know in your hearts that the FICA deduction from your paycheck is a big rip-off, but you hope that the day of reckoning will not come until after you've gotten yours. But if you are under 50, you may never see it, or it may be so inflation-ravaged that it won't buy much. It is by far the biggest Ponzi pyramid the mind of man has ever conceived, and, like all Ponzi schemes, it will see its day of reckoning.

Ponzi Revisited

A man by the name of Ponzi raised funds from investors by allegedly investing in heating oil and promising payoffs as high as forty percent a month. He bought no heating oil, did nothing productive with the money, and earned no real profits for his suckers, but he paid huge "dividends" to attract new investors *by using the money raised from other new investors!* The Ponzi pyramid eventually collapsed of its own weight, and Ponzi went to jail.

It's considered a crime when private citizens like Madoff do it, but it's "compassionate social engineering" when the government does it!

As long as enough new suckers pay into Social Security to balance the books, the fraud holds up. But if the number of paying "marks" diminishes due to a shrinking birth rate until they cannot or will not balance the books, the scheme collapses spectacularly.

Just understanding this truth may give you more incentive to begin preparing for a retirement that does *not* depend on Social Security—even if it *does* somehow hang together until you die. Congress and the Fed will just print money rather than raise taxes or cut benefits, so it is a lead-pipe cinch precursor of future inflation. You will be far better off when you retire if you don't bet on Social Security as it is now constituted.

Social Security was originally intended only to be an income supplement to your personal savings and other pensions. Under the most optimistic scenario, Social Security alone wouldn't allow you anything but genteel poverty when you can no longer earn a living.

In the most likely scenario, either Social Security won't even be there when you need it, or the money they will have to print to pay your monthly check will cause a saber-toothed inflation that will so diminish the purchasing power of the money that it will be worth much less in purchasing power.

And the politicians know it.

The Hard Truth of the Social Security Scam

The following exchange took place **25 years ago** during Senate Social Security hearings between Senator William Proxmire and a Mr. Cardwell of the Social Security Administration:

> **PROXMIRE**: *"There are 37 million people; is that right, who get Social Security benefits?"*

CARDWELL: *"Today between 32 million and 34 million."*

PROXMIRE: *"I'm a little high; 32 to 34 million people. Almost all of them or many of them are voters. In my state, I figure there are 600,000 voters that receive Social Security. Can you imagine a senator or congressman under those circumstances saying we are going to repudiate that high a proportion of the electorate? No.*

*Further, we have the capacity under the Constitution; the Congress does, 'to coin money' as well as to regulate the value thereof.' Therefore, we have the power to provide that money, and we are going to do it. **IT MAY NOT BE WORTH ANYTHING WHEN THE RECIPIENT GETS IT, BUT HE IS GOING TO GET HIS BENEFITS PAID."***
[emphasis added]

CARDWELL: *"I tend to agree!"*

I'm not so much worried that the Social Security system will utterly collapse but that the Social Security system will be one cause of the nation's bankruptcy through inflation. After Medicare, it is the second largest obligation of government.

Why Social Security Won't Ever Be Fixed

When I express my politically incorrect views on this subject, I rub a lot of people the wrong way. Social Security is a sacred cow that we are not supposed to question. It's called the Third Rail of Politics. When George Bush tried to mildly reform it, the Democrats clobbered him by raising false fears, and the Republicans ran for the hills. But as the saying goes, "Fools rush in where angels fear to tread." Call me a fool.

During the 2000 presidential campaign and the first few months of his administration, President Bush proposed that two percentage points of your FICA contribution be yours to invest in market securities at your option. Historically, that money would produce a return double the two percent yield you now get from Social Security and *the principal would be yours at retirement*! Gore and other Democrats immediately attacked this proposal as "a risky scheme," too vulnerable to market losses.

Here is the *truth* about why Congress will *never* fix Social Security before it is too late: it's a huge slush fund for government, and the big spenders will never let it out of their hands! Can you imagine what would happen to federal spending if suddenly the government could not borrow from the Social Security Trust Fund and spend it on their favorite programs? They'd be at least $175 billion short every year!

But remember, the Fed has a printing press primed to produce money. Inflation, anyone?

Total Unfunded Liabilities:
The Hyperinflationary Doomsday Machine

Social Security is only one part of America's astronomical inflationary liability. Don't forget Medicare, Medicaid, and all the other current and future entitlements dangling in front of American voters.

On March 20, 2007, a statement was made by *David M. Walker*, the Controller General of the United States, in a poorly attended

House sub-committee hearing. He said, "...*The federal government's financial condition and fiscal outlook are worse than many may understand*" [emphasis added].

At that time, he said the U.S. government's total reported liabilities, net social-insurance commitments, and other exposure (before Obama) "are now currently *over $50 trillion*" (that's trillion with a *T*). That represents approximately four times the nation's total output (GDP) in fiscal year 2006, up from about $20 trillion, or two times GDP, in fiscal year 2000.

Walker elaborates, "One way to think about it is: if we wanted to put aside today enough to cover these promises, it would take about *$440,000 per American household*, up from $190,000 in 2000. As these numbers indicate, the federal government faces large and growing structural deficits, primarily related to Medicare and other social-insurance commitments. These structural deficits, which are virtually certain, will mean escalating and *ultimately unsustainable deficits* and debt levels" [author's emphasis].

Did you get that? *The total of reported liabilities, contingencies, social insurance, and other commitments and promises soared from $20 trillion to about $50 trillion in just six years.* It's now $68 trillion in 2009 as this is written!

These figures guarantee a hyperinflationary future!

Will Congress raise taxes to pay for the entitlements? Not much.
Will it cut entitlement benefits? Never!
Will they print money? For sure!

PART III

PRESCRIPTIONS

CHAPTER 7

Ruffonomics:
ECONOMICS FOR MIDDLE-CLASS AMERICAN FAMILIES

I love the man that can smile in trouble,
that can gather strength from distress, and grow brave by reflection.
'Tis the business of little minds to shrink.
—Thomas Paine

*R**uffonomics* is a set of common-sense financial principles; a way of wisely making (and keeping) real wealth. It's not a dry academic subject for intellectual economists to debate nor is it a philosophy meant to compete with socialism, communism, libertarianism, Keynesianism, or Obamanomics. It doesn't tell government or Wall Street what to do, but rather informs middle-class Americans how they should conduct their financial lives in order to create their own personal economy which can then bypass the negative forces of Obamanomics in these difficult times. Ruffonomics makes your family the center of your personal economic universe.

Ruffonomics renders *Obamanomics* (which is synonymous with European-style socialism) virtually irrelevant. Ruffonomics runs counter to the conventional financial wisdom.

Ruffonomics consists of several principles:

1) It is **family oriented**. I have given the very same advice to my own family through the years, and I have a big one. It's natural for me to write for families because I spend a lot of time thinking about and serving my own large family. Family orientation comes naturally to me—and my wife, Kay, won't let me forget it.

2) Ruffonomics is **not designed to help rich people get richer**, although that could be a side benefit for well-to-do readers who apply the principles. These principles aren't just for the rich, and although some may join our cause, I don't expect these ideas to be widely accepted by big-time, money-motivated stock market investors.

   My advice has always been—and always will be—aimed at middle-class American families, just like yours.

3) Ruffonomics is based on **the constitution, capitalism, free enterprise,** and **old-fashioned morality**. A copy of the complete constitution hangs on the wall in my office. I believe the men who created it were inspired by God. (Unfortunately, the judges who interpret it now tend to substitute their own political and social judgments for these traditional principles. Judges are the referees of America and the constitution provides the rules of the game. These referees should strictly interpret the pre-existing rules, not make up their own.)

   I also believe in *capitalism*. Capitalism is a way to capitalize income by turning a private business into a public company whose value is generally determined by some multiple of profits. It's the way to create real wealth.

Free enterprise means you can start any business you want and enjoy the tangible rewards if you succeed—or take the knocks if you fail. It is diametrically opposed to Obamanomics, which fraudulently promises that you can succeed with no risk of failure, because the government is the Big Kahuna who will save you. Obamanomics generally appeals to both the college-based intellectuals and the less educated, non-productive bottom layer of American society. Its appeal is based on the false premise that your status in life is not your fault because you are just a victim of the Bad Guys (like us.)

4) Ruffonomics is **basically optimistic and forward-looking**. One of my favorite Broadway musicals, *Till the Clouds Roll By*, has a song with lyrics I love: "Look for the silver lining, when 'ere a cloud appears in the blue." I am basically optimistic, even though I seem to spend a lot of time viewing the country with alarm these days. That is only because I am rejecting the old financial world that is being ripped out from under us by Obamanomics.

I believe there are always opportunities to prosper if you know where to look, but in the Obama era, you won't find them in traditional institutions. If you share the Ruffonomics philosophy, you will *always* look for opportunities outside the mainstream. History is dynamic and ever changing. Fortunes are always made by those who detect these dramatic changes and bet on them early in the game while sticking to basic moral principles.

5) **Old-fashioned morals** are foundational. Traditional families with mom, dad and kids are the strength of America. They are currently under siege by the Sexual Anarchists, as described in chapter four.

6) Ruffonomics advises you to **get out of debt**. Debt is slavery. Many Americans send a huge chunk of their income each month to lenders who gave them money to purchase something that lost much of its value the minute they bought it. Now, too much of their money is committed to interest payments on another new car, a bigger house, a home theater, a vacation in an exotic place, a cruise, etc. They have no control over where their money goes. By contrast, those who have no debt can use their money at *their* discretion (often to make more money).

7) Ruffonomics tells you to be an investment maverick and **ignore Wall Street** in an economy like this. A maverick is a bovine that leaves the herd—perhaps one out of a thousand. The maverick may feel alone at times, but the rest of the herd will be turned into hamburger. The maverick at least has a chance! The maverick doesn't follow the herd and neither will those who practice Ruffonomics.

8) Ruffonomics suggests that because of Obamanomics, you should **invest in inflation**. Several investments *always* respond to inflation (See Chapter 12). At the right time, when the money supply is exploding as it is now, you should weight your portfolio in favor of inflation hedges. Some things respond directly to inflation (like gold and silver) and some simply respond to business opportunities in the inflationary environment. My life is a constant search for these unconventional opportunities. I then share them with you so you can select from a menu of wise investment options.

9) Ruffonomics is **not accepted** by those who believe in the conventional wisdom or who are fans of Barack Obama.

Ruffonomics tells you that most opportunities will be found in non-traditional areas. You can make a lot more money early in a trend than in a generally accepted, already established one. I look for those new trends.

CHAPTER 8

Old-Fashioned Family Values:
AMERICAN'S HIDDEN STRENGTH

Your success as a family, our success as a society, depends not on what happens at the White House, but what happens inside your house.
—Barbara Bush

Traditional families are the foundation of America. They were the pioneers who settled America as we moved westward. They cleared the arable land, planted the farms, and founded the businesses that became the core of America. Family values—a father and mother teaching children America's founding traditions and old-fashioned religious-based morals—*must* be restored to a place of honor in America.

As I've mentioned before, Kay and I have a great old-fashioned, big family—14 children (five adopted, mostly as teenagers) and 76 grandchildren—and nothing makes me happier. Citizens of many Third World countries consider children to be part of their wealth, as they can support their parents in their old age. Kay and I don't need to be supported because we are doing just fine, but our family's spiritual strength is our pride and joy. I consider my family a benefit for America, as they have learned to work hard and prosper in the American free-market, entrepreneurial system.

One of the major attacks on the family is demonizing people who have big families. When *How to Prosper During The Coming Bad Years* was first published, every once in a while I would go on a radio or TV show that cursed me for having a big family (our picture was on the back cover) that supposedly used more than our fair share of the earth's scarce resources.

The real problem is the exactly the opposite—families are too small. Western civilization has a demographic crisis. In Europe, the non-Muslim population is shrinking because they are having too few children to even replace themselves. By contrast, the Muslim families migrating into Europe are averaging eight children per family. This means that demographically they will eventually control Europe without firing a bullet or blowing up a neighborhood.

As the years go on, strong families will become even more important to America, especially as the socialist God fails. Family unity will be critical in the future. Organize your family so it is in tune with your values. Some family members may be richer than others, but if families unite, they can support one another. At no time in history has family unity been more important than it is now.

Family Matters

How did I organize my family? I didn't have a specific plan; it just happened based on my cultural conditioning. I bonded with them.

I'd like to share a few things that helped our family; I hope they'll help yours too. I'm a practicing Mormon (I'll keep practicing until I get it right), and that has shaped who I am and how I raised my family. Even though the theology of my church (The Church of Jesus Christ of Latter-day Saints or LDS Church, nicknamed "The Mormons") might be different from yours, it is built on a nineteenth-century, self-sufficiency culture you might agree with, even admire. Certain principles I learned at church are consistent with common pro-American values. You don't have to attend or join my church to believe in the things that helped Kay and me build a strong family. You can adapt them to your needs.

1) Since I was a child, my church taught me that **the Constitution is an inspired document**. Like me, my children were taught that the men who created the Constitution were inspired, raised up by God to do a historic work. Even if you don't believe the Constitution has divine origins, you can believe in its principles, practice them in your life, and teach them to your children.

2) Have a regular Family Home Evening. (This applies mostly to families with young children or teenagers.) Family Home Evening is an LDS church policy. You can call this Family Counsel if you like. We had one every Monday evening. At this Home Evening, we discussed problems that the whole family needed to be involved in, principles and values we wanted our children to understand, and some of my old-fashioned ideas about constitutional government and free enterprise. We didn't just deal with constitutional or free-market issues; we also dealt with the timeless issues of behavior and morality. These are things all families have in common, regardless of our religious heritage.

It didn't happen every Monday evening without exception, but it was pretty consistent. Our basic rule was that our children were not allowed to date nor have other activities on Family Home Evening night. If they wanted to be with their friends, their friends could attend our Family Home Evening. Sometimes I would conduct the meeting, sometimes Kay would, and sometimes one of the children would be assigned to teach a specific lesson.

It helps to have an overt, organized teaching process. I would suggest that any chapter of this book would be a great subject for a Family Home Evening.

3) Be a sermon. Someone once said, "Your life may be the only sermon anyone will ever hear." My children were able to look at their mother and me and see us practice what we believed. I didn't have to preach to them about morals and constitutional government. They just saw what I was living. I also made sure they all had *The Ruff Times* to read so when I made a point to my subscribers, it was also to my children. I didn't need to always be overtly preaching.

4) Never stop being a parent. Now that we have many grandchildren and great-grandchildren, I know I can go on any Monday night to one of our children's homes and get in on a Family Home Evening as an honored guest, sometimes even being asked to conduct the meeting. Sometimes they might simply come to our house on a Monday night and conduct their Family Home Evening with us. Seeing this, I know our values have been adopted and practiced, and this unites us.

6) Love your children's mother. The most important gift a man can give his children is to love their mother. I showed my love for Kay always, and the children knew there was no question about it.

It gave them a sense of stability which helped to unite us and bring us together.

7) Start a family organization. You could start a family foundation and the older children could contribute cash to be made available when any member of the family comes into hard times. Perhaps they could contribute money and vote on a cause they could give money to. The important thing is that you are united in purpose.

8) Travel together. I remember how we went to Europe to pick up my son, Larry, when he finished his LDS mission in France. Five of our children went with us. We had a wonderful time touring Europe in a VW Wagon.

9) Have a bonding activity. Our bonding activity was always fishing. I taught all the kids to fish. We caught and ate a lot of fish together. We enjoyed a fifty foot houseboat on Lake Powell (in Southern Utah). We would always fish, and several of our meals on the boat were prepared from the fish we caught.

10) Give each child a special trip. We always celebrated either the eighth or twelfth birthday by taking them on a business trip with Dad. I remember going to New York City with my adopted son, Anthony as a teenager. In between meetings with my publisher and staying over an extra day, Anthony and I just toured the city. Anthony was impressed with St. Patrick's magnificent cathedral. We went to the top of the Empire State Building and traveled around in a tour bus. We bought souvenirs to bring home and share with the family. It was an important part of my bonding with Anthony.

11) Genealogy. Acquaint all of your children with your ancestors so they know you didn't just spring up like a weed. My children know who my parents and grandparents and other ancestors were. Some of my ancestors have written their histories, and we have given copies to our children to read.

12) Share your profession. Let your children know what you do every day. I share mine by letting them read *The Ruff Times*. You can do this by taking your children one at a time to the office with you, or taking them on the aforementioned business trips. Sit down with them and explain the problems you are dealing with in your work. It helps them bond to you and understand why you are sometimes preoccupied.

13) Above all, give them time. I've heard a lot about quality time as opposed to quantity time. Quality time matters, but quantity time matters too.

I remember my friend who was the CEO of a Fortune 500 company. He became one of Ronald Regan's appointees, heading the Commission on Government Waste. He performed wonderful services for the country and became one of my heroes.

When I invited him to be on my radio show in Salt Lake City, he hopped in his company 727, flew to Salt Lake City, and I interviewed him.

After the interview, he surprised me by asking, "Howard, do your children hate you?"

After I recovered from the shock, I said, "No, we have good relationships with our children. Do your children hate you?"

He said, "Yes, some of them won't even let me see my grandchildren."

Then we changed the subject.

He invited me to fly with him to Asia. I was already going to Bangkok, and I would have met up with his plane in Anchorage when they refueled. I asked if his wife would be with us.

He said, "Yes, but she understands she is not to bother me on trips because I take my management team with me and we work all the time. I don't have time for her, so she always brings a friend so she will have someone to talk to and travel with."

Uh-huh . . .

I then understood why he had no relationship with his children. The end result of it all was that when he died there was a vicious legal battle over his will and his wealth. They didn't care about him; they only cared about his money. As good a man as he was, as much good as he did (and he did a lot of good), he had failed the biggest test.

Succeed at Home

An LDS church leader once said, "No other success can compensate for failure in the home." I believe that with all my heart. I can honestly tell you that as our children have gotten older and have built their own families, we have maintained warm personal relationships. I have one daughter who is about as left-leaning politically and philosophically as you can imagine, but has a great and generous heart. She has traveled to Latin America and changed the lives of several poor people. Even if she doesn't share our religious and political philosophy, we have made it very clear that we love her. And she loves her mom and dad, despite their old-fashioned views.

81

I freely admit that I talk a better fight than I walk. We haven't been perfect. There have been times when we have been estranged for awhile from a couple of our children. But we continued to love them and expressed it often, and sooner or later they came back into the fold—maybe not into the church, but into the family fold. The most satisfying part of this is that I have watched them pass the same values onto their children, both by their personal behavior and by overt teaching.

You won't succeed with every child. There will be some failures and some breakups and some hostility. But you can avoid much of that if you just do the simple things I've mentioned, and, above all, tell each family member they are loved and appreciated.

Throughout the years when hard times came to our family, it was much easier to organize and pull together because we were bonded and shared common values.

I wish nothing less for you and your family.

CHAPTER 9

Getting Out of Debt:
WHY DEBT IS THE NEW SLAVERY

A man in debt is so far a slave.
—Ralph Waldo Emerson

The hard-earned income you are now sending to lenders is a lost opportunity. It's money that *could* be used more productively (to invest in inflation, to build commodity storage, to provide a cushion for you and your family, etc.) *if* it were available. You can't build real wealth if you are mired in debt.

A Dissertation on Debt

Debt is a way of life for most Americans. It seems next to impossible to avoid, simply because almost anyone will loan you money to satisfy any transitory impulse. Debt and consumer spending are now considered positive economic indicators, and government policy is openly aimed at stimulating consumer debt.

A lot of people will argue that debt is good for us. If it weren't for debt, you wouldn't have a home theater, a second car, a bigger house, etc. It helps create a nicer lifestyle, but it's an *artificial* lifestyle.

Debt is slavery with a nice face. After you incur a debt to buy something, you will have to send off money every month to pay for it—plus interest.

If enough people avoided debt, perhaps it might set a new, lower level of economic performance in America. Yes, if everyone decided to stop buying so much and instead started paying off debt, it would have short-term ill effects on the economy, but in the long run it would create a solid, sound base on which we could built. If each citizen's financial life is sound, America is sound. Avoiding debt is highly desirable in the long run.

Here's a personal illustration of the flawed logic surrounding debt in America. I once attended a "Father of the Year" award dinner for a man who has since passed away. He had owned several automobile dealerships and was one of the most successful businessmen in the state. He and I had been partners in the Utah Jazz way back when, and he eventually ended up as the sole owner. Everyone knew his name. He had good moral values and lived his religion. He was generous with his fortune. He was a good man.

Ironically, because of his auto dealerships and heavy advertising of new cars, he was also responsible for putting more people in debt than anyone else in Utah. He made a fortune encouraging debt. He sold people new cars when a two or three-year-old car would have got them from here to there sitting in air conditioned comfort just as well and would have spared them the slavery of high monthly payments.

When the recent recession hit, some of our neighbors and friends lost their jobs. Those who had accepted the counsel of our church leaders to avoid debt were okay. When I offered them financial help, they told me they had no need of my help. They had savings, and they could live on a much lower scale because they didn't have any debt repayments hanging over them.

In contrast, those who were obligated to monthly payments were in danger of losing everything, including financial freedom. Supporting your family is always easier when you have no debt. You can have discretion over your money, rather than committing it to lenders.

How to Get Out of Debt

First, adopt a whole new perspective toward possessions. You have to step down your standard of living and start saying no instead of yes. It's so hard to say no when borrowing and financing are so easy, but learn to be content with a smaller home, a two-or-three-year-old car, a smaller TV, etc. Accustom yourself to living on a simpler scale.

Kay and I practice what we preach. We bought a three-year-old Toyota Avalon. It's every bit as comfortable, attractive, and useful as a brand new car.

Second, quit comparing based on appearances. Your neighbors may have a bigger house with a new Mercedes and a boat in the driveway, but that doesn't prove they are richer (or wiser) than you. It just might prove they are more in debt. Just because other people are stupid with their money doesn't mean you should be.

Adopting a comfortable yet moderate, debt-free lifestyle over the next few years will be critical to your long-term financial success.

After You Are Out of Debt

What should you do with your discretionary money now that it is has been freed up from debt? *Prepare for—and invest in—inflation.*

After you are out of debt, you can't just leave your money in cash dollars because the dollar is headed for the dustbin of history. Dollars may eventually become more worthless than toilet paper (at least toilet paper absorbs water).

Money is supposed to be: **1)** a means of exchange, and **2)** a store of value. The dollar is still a means of exchange, but it has ceased to be a store of value.

Having no debt gives you control over your money, and leaves you with discretionary cash. If you put it in a bank, you are exposed to two dangers: **1)** the bank might go broke; and **2)** the money is going broke. You must change it into something that will hold its value.

There are better, easier ways to store the value of your assets. Reduce your dollar holdings to only that which is necessary for the orderly conduct of your business and family, and don't put it in a bank. Credit Unions are safer. Don't tie it up in long-term CDs. Invest your assets in inflation hedges. (Read Chapter 12 for more on this.)

One *Ruff Times* subscriber recently argued, "Perhaps you should have as much debt as possible. Then after runaway hyperinflation sets in, you can pay off your debts with worthless money." That sounds great in theory, but I'd rather be free to buy inflation hedges *today* so that money will retain its value and even grow tomorrow.

Beating Inflation at the Store

Due to inflation and the inevitable subsequent price controls, every store from which you buy goods on a regular basis will have trouble keeping the shelves stocked. When the price of oil soars over $100 per barrel again (and it will), truckers will have difficulty affording gasoline and diesel oil, and they won't show up at the back doors of the stores as often to restock the shelves. When that happens, you won't be able to count on buying what you want, when you want, at a price you want. Products will not disappear entirely, they will just become scarcer, much more expensive, and with less variety. This is always the result of socialist inflation, price controls, and shortages.

When I say "commodities," I don't just mean food (the most important commodity of all), but also diapers, soap, motor oil, fertilizer, medicine and everything else you need and use every day.

When you buy tuna, don't just buy a can, buy a case and store it. You will have bought at today's low prices and will consume at tomorrow's higher prices (buy low, consume high). Storing basic commodities will be one of the smartest protections against inflation you can make for your family.

CHAPTER 10

Entrepreneurism:
THE GUTS OF AMERICA

*I studied the lives of great men and famous women,
and I found that the men and women who got to the top
were those who did the jobs they had in hand, with everything
they had of energy and enthusiasm and hard work.*
—Harry S. Truman

As unemployment rises and it dawns on a lot of smart people that there is no real safety in working for a big corporation, many entrepreneurial startups will be born. True, many of these entrepreneurial ventures will be out of sheer desperation because people have lost their jobs and there are no job alternatives, but that could be a blessing in disguise.

The value of entrepreneurialism was brought home to me when I was in Hong Kong back in the '50s. A lot of Chinese had floated down the river from China into Hong Kong Bay, covering their heads with boxes so they wouldn't be seen, intercepted, and shot. They would then get an orange crate and either buy or steal some small commodities (fruits and vegetables or maybe some gadgets) and set up a small shop on a street corner. It eventually gave birth to many big companies. The irrepressible Chinese entrepreneurial urge turned Hong Kong into one of the great free markets of the world. Desperate Chinese refugees eventually built many multi-million dollar fortunes.

Similarly, when Kay and I were in South America, we met with a man who had written a popular book on the "shadow economy," which was the "unregulated" underground economy, started by entrepreneurs avoiding regulations and confiscatory taxation. It was this shadow economy that kept many of these countries afloat, because the real business took place underground.

The American Spirit of Enterprise

The American entrepreneur is the same breed of cat. I believe the entrepreneurial spirit will always flourish in this country, regardless of what the government does. It's true that the government can make the economic climate more or less business-friendly, but it can never snuff out the spirit that built this country.

Many friends who have recently lost their jobs with big companies are now starting businesses of their own. Most people think you need investors and money to start businesses, but you can market yourself into financial success on a shoestring, like the Chinese entrepreneurs did. You don't need a college education either. Many people without the required college degree have started successful ventures.

Maybe it's like my friend, Luzon, who set up a child day-care for preschoolers in her home. It supported their family when her husband lost his job. Maybe it's like my son, Eric, who with his brother, David, started a software company that they sold for millions. Maybe it's like my son-in-law, Scott, who started a software company and is rapidly building it into a successful venture. Maybe it is like Eric, who after selling the software company for a great profit founded a successful company that manufactures scrapbooking tools.

Security vs. Opportunity

Some time ago when I spoke to a church group, one woman raised her hand and said, "What do you do if your husband has to be an entrepreneur, but you want safety and security?"

I told her that half of the people in America want safety and security, the other half want opportunity, and the two halves tend to marry each other.

I'm grateful there are non-entrepreneurial, security-seeking people willing to work for me. I don't know what we would do in America if we didn't have people who will do the things the entrepreneur doesn't want to do, or even can't do. It takes both to make a business work.

In reality though, there is no such thing as guaranteed financial security. Some people think more government regulation of Corporate America means more safety, but the opposite is true. We have just found out in 2008 and 2009 that there is no security for anyone in big corporations. I know people who made handfuls of money as big-time corporate executives but still lost their jobs.

"Laissez faire" means literally "leave me alone," and that's what government *should* do with business. They won't though, and over the next few years, Obamanomics will attempt to bring everyone into the big government controlled corporate mold.

Risks and Rewards

Many entrepreneurs who have taken big risks and then earn big rewards are among the "rich" who have been vilified by the Obama administration. Many of these "rich" started out with one small store and then took their company public. After years of struggle and depriving their families of immediate benefits, they become an "instant success."

Now, they will be forced to pay confiscatory tax rates. As a result, the gold in the pot at the end of the rainbow is turning into brass. As the potential reward shrinks, fewer people will want to try.

The political tax attack on "the rich" is bad for America. Who will venture and sacrifice to build a company if they know that the government will tax away their profits when they do succeed? The attack on "the rich" is a preemptive assault on successful entrepreneurs. It will result in fewer new companies, which translates into fewer new jobs. It's a direct attack on the American Dream.

Even still, hard-working entrepreneurs can prosper in spite of Obamanomics and continue to breath life into the American economy, even during hard times.

Surmounting Obstacles

When I owned the Jefferson Institute, we conducted regular Entrepreneur Boot Camps. Nearly all attendees owned their own small companies. I once asked them, "How many of you have ever had your back to the wall, the wolf at your heels and burglars ready to break in, and it looked like you would never survive?"

Every hand in the room went up. What made the difference is that they stuck it out. They didn't give up and walk away. Some had failed at least once. The road to entrepreneurial success is often paved with failures.

Lessons from Art Linkletter

My friend, Art Linkletter, who was one of the most successful capitalists and entrepreneurs in Hollywood, once taught me a great lesson.

I asked, "Art, what's the secret of your success?"

Art said, "Howard, I have invested in a lot of startups. Some of them were successful and we would sell them at a profit. We would fly in our jets, take our checks, drink Champagne, sleep off the hangover, and then fly home. Today, I don't even know what those companies were.

"But if a company failed, I spent weeks literally rubbing my nose through the wreckage to find out why. Did we have a bad marketing plan? Were we undercapitalized? Why did we fail?

"Howard, I learned more from any one failure than I learned from all the successes."

Entrepreneurial failures are temporary setbacks on the way to success. It is rare than an entrepreneur gets an idea, makes it a success, and doesn't have at least one failure along the way.

Some years ago, I wrote a *Ruff Times* article on entrepreneurialism that became a classic. I've reprinted it several times before, but I'd like to share it here again.

* * * *

Seed Money: No Back Doors

Several times each month, I'm approached by friends with a new business idea, an invention or some special skill they want to sell. They usually want two things: money and advice. I never give them money, but if time permits, I give them my best advice, but not the usual balance sheet, marketing and financial-projection advice—all of which are, of course, important. The guts of business success are *the character, attitude and behavior of the entrepreneur.*

The successful entrepreneur is truly another breed of cat. He has a compulsion for growth and success. He happily takes carefully calculated risks and the road to success is often paved with a failure or two.

Here's my list of the things you must have to achieve business success, "Ruffly" in descending order of importance. Without most of them, you won't make it. You might still make it without one or two of them, but the odds are against it.

1) A supportive spouse

Nothing is more destructive to a marriage or a business than a spouse who is not willing to endure years of deprivation, chronic cash shortages and fear (the sky-is-falling feeling when you wake up at 4:00 a.m.). Needed is an almost Christ-like willingness to refrain from nagging or criticism when success takes longer than expected. Without that attitude, the emotional price to be paid will often cause either the marriage or the business to fail.

If your spouse adds unnecessary emotional burdens to the already intolerable, new-business pressures, you will be less effective. Or, in your desire to please your spouse, you cannot, or will not, make the sacrifices necessary for success.

Kay was always totally supportive. She believed in me with all her heart, and did her best to make home a heaven on Earth. Without the support of your spouse, a new business is usually dead meat.

2) No Back Doors

Starting a small business is an all-consuming, frustrating, and exhausting effort. If you have an easy out, a terrific job to go back to, a lot of cash to fall back on, or whatever, you probably won't hang in there when it is tempting to give up.

Almost every successful business had occasions when all seemed lost. The guy who refused to give up made it.

If you have a back door, you are much more likely to quit when it seems hopeless. If you really want to succeed in business, burn your bridges so there is only one way to go, and that's forward. A kamikaze is more likely to complete his mission if the wheels fall off as he takes off, which the Japanese did in World War II.

3) Incurable Optimism

Small businesses rarely succeed when the financial guy is a pessimist, or overly cautious with an "accountant-like mentality." I'm not knocking accountants. Not all of them have "accountant-like mentalities." I mean the timid souls who always see problems where the entrepreneur sees opportunities.

When a real entrepreneur sees an opportunity, he pounces on it. If he keeps his eye on his objective, obstacles are merely exciting challenges. He believes in himself, his product, and his mission, despite everyone else's pessimism.

Napoleon Hill's great book, *Think and Grow Rich* says, "No great enterprise will ever begin if all obstacles must first be overcome." That is the entrepreneur's creed. Optimism ultimately prevails because skepticism eventually crumbles under the relentless pressure of an incurable optimist. Nobody will follow a skeptic very far. The optimists sweep others away with their enthusiasm and spur them to greater performance heights by giving them a sense of mission. An optimist has to hire some pessimists to keep the books and deal with the banker, but he should keep them out of his life as much as possible because they will stifle his dream.

There's an utterly hilarious movie you all should see called "The Gods Must Be Crazy." It's the delightful story of an African Bushman family in a remote part of the Kalahari Desert. They have no possessions, living happily and simply until a passing private pilot throws a coke bottle out of his plane and it is picked up by a bushman.

It's the only possession his family has ever had, and soon they're squabbling for the first time in the history of their family, so the father decides to go to the end of the world and throw off the bottle.

A subplot involves a game biologist who is delivering a pretty schoolteacher to her job in Botswana. Along the way, they start a small campfire. Suddenly, a rhinoceros comes rushing in and stamps out the fire.

Apparently, rhinos are Africa's self-appointed fire-control officers. When they see a small fire, they run in and stamp it out. I know that sounds incredible, but after you've seen the movie, you'll believe.

Optimistic entrepreneurs must not surround themselves with rhinos that stamp out their creative fires. The skeptics will try to stamp out your ideas while they are still fragile. Keep away from them until the fire of your dream is a raging conflagration no rhino can stamp out. Then you can safely involve the accountants, attorneys, and other skeptics who can help you control your fires without endangering your blazing dream.

A start-up business without incurable optimism will die.

4) *The Ability to Postpone Gratification*

The budding entrepreneur must be willing to deprive himself now to get the big rewards later. If he insists on taking a big salary out of the budding business, he will suck it dry before it matures.

When my sons bring me a new business plan with a big salary for themselves, I toss it back. They won't have the sense of desperation that forces them to land the contract *now*, to make that sale *now*, to rush the project to completion *now*.

Postponement of gratification is the surest sign of maturity. Many successful entrepreneurs eventually live high lifestyles—big cars, big houses, flashy rings, etc.—as the postponed payoff for years of deprivation when they hardly knew what they were going to eat, let alone which car to buy. They enjoy it to the fullest when rewards come, because they paid the price first. Perhaps this satisfies some subconscious need to flaunt their success before the cynics who said it couldn't be done—rubbing their noses in it as a sort of delicious revenge. The conspicuous consumption is understandable after the years of self-denial (and very common).

5) Intellectual Honesty

The real entrepreneur has a delicate balance between rampant optimism and realism. He admits when his product falls short of expectations and needs to be improved.

When he looks at accounting numbers, he doesn't allow his optimism to cloud his good judgment. He faces his problems and deals with them, while never allowing his problems to convince him that "it ain't gonna work." Because he is honest with himself, he's also honest with others. When he hires people, he candidly lays out the risks and rewards, but his optimism still shines through.

He relies on his accountant for real numbers, but doesn't allow those numbers to destroy his dream when they look bleak, because he believes that through hard work and ingenuity, he can change them. But he faces the truth as it is.

If he isn't intellectually honest, sooner or later some fact he refused to face will rise up and bite him. Optimism won't save him if it is built on the sand of unfaced facts.

Pessimists distort this principle to justify their pessimism. They say "Here are the facts. It's terrible. There's nothing you can do about it. Give up."

The intellectually honest optimist says, "Here are the facts. I acknowledge that, but I can change them, and I will."

6) A Friend or Partner

Usually the entrepreneur has skills in one or two areas, but is woefully lacking in others. He might be a great salesman, but knows nothing about production or accounting. He might be an electronics genius or inventor who couldn't sell worms to fishermen, and to him, accounting is witchcraft.

He needs a business associate who shares his dream and supplies the skills he does not have. All my major successes have been shared with such a partner.

When I started my Reading Dynamics school (which, despite my subsequent failure, was very successful for several years), I shared my dreams with John Manson who believed in them and helped me execute them.

When I founded *The Ruff Times* in 1975, I had Terry Jeffers, an administrator and computer expert from IBM. I concentrated on reading, writing and marketing, and Terry ran the business.

I could dump my dreams all over Terry and John, and they reinforced and supported them. They weren't fire-control rhinos and they believed in me. They supplied skills that enabled me to concentrate on what I do best.

One of my most important business strategies is to assess my deficiencies and my strengths, then spend my time doing only the things I do best. That takes intellectual honesty. I either hire or affiliate with people who can do the things I do not do well. Once you honestly acknowledge that you don't do something well, and turn those things over to competent people who can share your dream, you are unleashed.

Some people have a strong enough ego to stand alone, but most of us do a heck of a lot better with someone shoulder to shoulder with us, to plug the holes in our defenses.

7) A Strong Ego

I don't know any successful businessman who isn't an egotist, although some are better than others at concealing it. There is a crucial difference between a big, strong ego and a big, fragile one. I know some very talented people in my business that offend easily and are constantly on the alert for slights and insults, real or imagined.

The person with a strong ego simply shrugs off most criticism and only counter-attacks when good business judgment says he must. He usually just sails serenely on his self-confident way.

My ego is at least as big as anyone in my business. Without it, I never would have believed that my deathless prose or unorthodox economic views were worth charging for, but I can honestly say I rarely let that ego affect my business judgment. Whenever I have, I have failed.

The clearest symptom of a strong, secure ego is the ability to laugh when the joke is on you, to take a lot of kidding without pain, and to never doubt yourself, despite the ridicule of the majority.

I know my ego rubs some people wrong, but being 78 years old, I seriously doubt if my personality will change much. My family helps me keep my ego under some control. If Dad gets too pompous, my kids are wonderfully creative at bringing me down to earth. Around the Ruff House, the joke was usually on me.

Only a person with a secure ego will face reality, admit mistakes, cut losses and change directions. A strong ego reflects itself in many ways, some of them rather obnoxious, but usually the braggart or the temperamental artist has a fragile ego, not a strong one.

Here's a true definition of temperamental: nine-tenths temper and one-tenth mental.

Secondary, But Still Important

Here are a few more points which may not be as fundamental as the above, but can increase the success odds of a small business:

1) *You need a business plan*

A business plan isn't just an idea or a narrative. It's a concept reduced to numbers on a month-by-month projection. It realistically projects monthly expenditures and income for two years, and quarterly.

Without a business plan, you don't have the slightest idea of whether or not your project is even worth doing. You don't know how much capital you need or where your potential pitfalls are.

A good business plan is revised constantly as the real numbers come in and become more and more accurate. Without a business plan, you need a lot more luck, which leads me to point number two.

2) *You need a computer*

You need a personal computer to run that spread sheet. Back in the days before PC's, I remember sitting laboriously hour after hour with my adding machine and my accounting paper, cranking in all of the assumptions about sales and expenses. If I changed one assumption, I had to redo the whole spread sheet. I don't know how many pencils and erasers I wore out. I also remember stopping from sheer exhaustion before I had all the answers I needed.

A PC can change all the other numbers with a keystroke when you change one assumption. A business without a computer spread sheet business plan can succeed, but it is infinitely easier with a personal computer.

3) You need a "position"

A position is a simple concept that aims for a relatively narrow segment of the market. When people bring me business deals, they often emphasize how this is "for everyone." Successful businesses usually found a relatively narrow market segment and had a relatively simple product or service. The right name or advertising slogan automatically defines that position.

One example of positioning was Free the Eagle's fight against the IMF funding several years ago. Our position was simple. "They're bailing out the big banks with your tax money." Not only was it true, but it clicked into place in people's heads and it was very difficult to drive out. That simple position won the battle of public opinion. The IMF only got their money because the President gave the Democrats a $14 billion housing bill to buy fifty votes in the House.

The more specific and specialized your product or service, the more likely it is to be successful. In this great nation, even a narrowly focused concept should be big enough to make you rich. A concept which tries to be all things to all people is a hundred pound marshmallow. No one knows where to start eating. It generally does not cause people to flock to your door.

You can broaden your concept later, but only within your position.

Intangibles

This lengthy treatise has dealt mostly with intangibles, but intangibles rule the world.

Hitler didn't lead Germany because he was a good manager or accountant. He led it with charisma and the intangible force of his twisted dream, which almost destroyed western civilization.

On the other hand, Jesus had an intangible dream that motivated people to face death and torture or to change their lives, and He changed the world.

Obama won the election with a huge majority. His secret? He convinced voters he represented "change." Those who were unhappy with things as they were flocked to him. They didn't know what "change" meant, but they bought it. (We gave his administration trillion of dollars, and he gave us back the change!)

Intangible principles are the difference between business success and failure. As Mark McCormack points out in his book *What They Don't Teach You at the Harvard Business School*, business schools are numbers-oriented, systems-oriented, and computer-oriented.

That's fine, but those tangibles can never take the place of a powerful idea. Without it, to quote an old southern friend of mine, "That dog won't hunt."

The Backbone of America

Small business entrepreneurs are the backbone of America. They are the future Google and Microsoft. They are people with an idea, a dream, and the drive to turn it into something. They have built companies that have provided most of the jobs in America. We must honor these start-up entrepreneurs and tax them less when they succeed.

If you want more entrepreneurism and more successful small ventures that grow into big ones, just remember this basic principle: if you want less of something, tax it; if you want more of something, cut their taxes so they keep the rewards of their efforts. Basically, entrepreneurism is and will be the great future of America. It can save America from the catastrophe that Obamanomics will lead us into.

CHAPTER 11

How To Lose Money In a Hurry:

WHAT FINANCIAL POISON TO AVOID

We are apt to shut our eyes against a painful truth...
For my part, I am willing to know the whole truth;
to know the worst; and to provide for it.

—Patrick Henry

Over the years, I've prided myself not so much on the investments that made money, but on the bad investments readers avoided on which they could have taken a bath if they hadn't been warned. Now is a time just like that.

Conventional wisdom can beat down your portfolio in the age of Obama. Remember, only the mavericks that don't follow the herd will make money because the herd will get slaughtered.

Avoid at All Costs:

1) Growth stocks and growth mutual funds

These will suffer in the age of Obamanomics because America's growth will come to a near-screeching halt. There will be some short-term opportunities (as there always are, even under the worst circumstances), but as a category, it is best to avoid them.

You can bet against the stock market by buying *Rydex Inverse S&P 500 Strategy Inv (RYURX)*. This mutual fund is counter-cyclical to the S&P 500.

2) Bonds and most other fixed-interest investments

When interest rates rise (and they will because of Obamanomics-induced inflation), fixed-return investments go down. T-bonds are especially dangerous. They are considered the most "conservative" and are fundamental to the recommendations made by most financial advisors when times get tough; yet these investments will be hurt the most. You can also buy *Rydex Inverse Government Long Bond Strategy Inv (RYJUX)*. It is counter-cyclical to bonds; it will go up when bonds go down.

If you need income, avoid most bonds and utility stocks. Instead, consider *Canadian Oil and Gas Trusts* listed in *The Ruff Times Investment Menu* in each issue of *The Ruff Times*. Some yield between *twelve and twenty-five percent*. They will prosper over the years ahead and pay you remarkable dividends.

Call Jim Raby at 800-431-4488. He's my broker.

3) *Money-market funds*

Money-market funds are not investments, even in good times; they are simply temporary places to park your money while you decide where to deploy it. Money-market funds may not go broke, but the dollar *will*. Limit your exposure to the dollar, and that means avoid money-market funds as much as possible.

Use a credit union, but only for that cash which is necessary for the orderly conduct of your personal or business affairs. You can't avoid dollars entirely, but you can limit your exposure to them.

4) *Golden Frauds*

During gold bull markets, like the present, crooks realize that gold has a great emotional appeal. Many decisions to buy gold are made by unsophisticated, often elderly people who don't have a guide like this one. These frauds are a combination of poor business practices and downright lies. Let me cover the most common:

1) **The leveraged purchase.** Some coin dealers have discovered that they can talk you into committing to buy several times more metal by simply telling you that rather than just paying one hundred percent for gold or silver, you can take the same dollars to pay ten percent and own ten times as much gold. This seems attractive, because you feel you have multiplied your potential profits by ten—unless the market turns down in a short-term correction, which it is wont to do. That can wipe out your margin and you will get a margin call. If you don't meet it, they will sell you out, and you lose all your money.

2) **Storing your gold for you.** Some companies will advise you to buy gold from them and store it with them or invest in "pool accounts." You have no way to tell if they actually bought the metal.

An exception might be one of my recommended vendors, *Investment Rarities*, which has a relationship with *Brinks* that will store metal for you. There are real safeguards, such as serial numbers on all gold and silver bars. You can also visit your metal any time you want, or pick it up and take possession. The trustees are independent of any profits accruing to Investment Rarities for selling you the metal.

3) **Futures contracts and options.** Besides the dangers I mentioned above, there are always sharpies who will want you to buy futures contracts or options. Most of the money you put down will go to commissions. It is simply a rip off of your pocketbook for an over-priced contract.

4) **Other frauds.** Other new frauds will certainly arise. Every hot investment market throughout history has had its own frauds, sometimes inherent in the very nature of the investment, and sometimes by manipulation by scoundrels. Gold is no exception. Stick to my Recommended Vendors or go to your neighborhood coin shop and pick up the metal and take it home with you. That's the only way to be absolutely sure. Play it safe and take my advice. And always compare prices, even with my Recommended Vendors.

In Chapter 12, I'll teach you exactly what you *should* invest in.

Thinking Outside The Box:
MAVERICK INVESTING IN THE AGE OF OBAMANOMICS

*You are not here merely to make a living. You are here to enrich the
world, and you impoverish yourself if you forget the errand.*
—Woodrow Wilson

T he most important thing you need to know about investing in
the Age of Obamanomics is: *invest in inflation.*

Consider two key investments that are perfect for the Age of
Obamanomics: precious metals and carefully selected stocks. When
we're done with this chapter, you'll know exactly what to look for and
how to avoid the pitfalls.

Your investment program should be based in coins and bullion.
Invest at least one-third of your assets in gold and silver coins or bars.

Precious Metals Are Basic to a Ruffonomics Portfolio

Gold and silver are perfect pure inflation hedges. Strictly seen
as an investment, as the dollar shrinks in value, gold will be worth

thousands of dollars an ounce and silver will be worth hundreds of dollars an ounce. Glenn Beck, one of my favorite talk show hosts, said he is "not buying gold as an investment, although it will be a good investment, but as insurance." He doesn't tell us what he is insuring against, but I'll tell you. He's insuring against the plummeting loss of purchasing power of all dollar-denominated investments, even the possible collapse of the dollar.

Precious metals feel so solid. When I was in South Africa, I went ten thousand feet down in a gold mine, and then came up to visit where they were producing gold bars. I held a new gold bar in my hands. It felt like wealth. It was real.

Then I went to the mint that manufactured krugerrands, South African gold coins, and we were permitted to handle these coins. Same feelings. I understand why people killed for them.

Why Gold and Silver Now?

In these current circumstances, not buying gold or silver is one of the dumbest money decisions you can make in 2009-2010. Here are just a few reasons why this is so:

1) Obamanomics

Socialist states *always inflate* the paper currency. Obama, Congress, and the Federal Reserve are diluting the dollar like never before by creating more of it. Accommodating Obama and Congress, the Fed has manufactured trillions of dollars out of nothing at by far the fastest pace in history, and it's accelerating. The government has given trillions to the big banks, which will loan the dollars into circulation or give them to politicians to spend into circulation. This money expansion currently dwarfs several times over the monetary explosion that led to the Carter-driven metals bull market in the '70s.

I can't overstate what is happening. Economists may call this monetary-expansion process "inflation" but it really should be called "dilution"—dilution of the money supply and consequently its value. Inevitably, sooner or later, consumer prices rise and laymen then mistakenly call that "inflation." Calling rising prices inflation is like calling falling trees hurricanes.

When will the public catch on? Price inflation and gold prices are the chief measurements of public awareness. Sooner or later, awareness becomes a critical mass, the public catches on, and the metals go through the stratosphere.

2) *Real money*

Gold and silver (especially silver) have been real money over and over again, in all ages of time and on all continents. Ever since Gutenberg invented the printing press 400 years ago, the world has been littered with worthless dead paper currencies every seventy-five to eighty years, due to runaway money printing. *Every time* the dominant currency has been inflated, gold and silver coins have become hugely profitable investments, and sometimes the only surviving currency.

Throughout history, each time a paper currency finally caved in to inflation, gold and silver (especially silver) became the only universally acceptable coin of the realm. Gold and silver as a means of exchange and a store of value have always survived. They have always been symbols of wealth, far more precious in our consciousness than any mere paper.

During periods of hyperinflation, there always comes a time when people refuse to accept more and more counterfeit, inflated money or base-metal coins in return for their hard-produced goods and services. At that point, society instinctively turns to gold and silver. It has happened over and over again, and as George Santayana said, "Those who can not remember the past are condemned to repeat it."

3) It's early in the game

Gold and silver are *early in an historic bull market* (in fact, as this is written, it's only a Golden Calf), making this a low-risk investment with an awesome upside for the long-term investor. Especially silver. This gold and silver bull market will dwarf the last great one in 1973-80, when fortunes were made by relatively small amounts of money invested by amateur investors (many of them my readers). All of the factors that created the last bull market are here again, only amplified several times.

4) Supply and demand

Both metals are far more rare than most people know. All the gold ever mined since the dawn of history, including that in Central banks, gold fillings, and sunken shipwrecks in the Caribbean, etc. would cover a football field about four-feet deep. It would make a cube about the size of a typical 8-room house. Demand is now leaping past new supplies.

Likewise, most of the easy silver has been mined over the centuries, even with primitive methods. For example, during the Roman millennium, they used silver coins for currency and exhausted the Spanish silver mines.

Now that prices are high enough to make gold and silver mining profitable again, it will take as much as seven to ten years to develop new mines, and stagnant supply and rising demand have made higher prices inevitable for the imminent future.

Food for Thought

In 1980 the historic '70s gold bull market finally topped out at $850. After adjusting for inflation, to merely equal what it did in 1980, gold would have to go (only) to $2,300, and silver topped out at $50 in 1980. After adjusting for inflation since then, to merely make a new high, silver would have to go over $125 and gold to $2,300!

Why might the metals go even higher? Most compelling is the fact that the biggest single factor that drives gold and silver is monetary inflation, and that's already several times greater now than it was during the great gold-and-silver bull market of the '70s. In fact, gold and silver have been rising in response to money creation since 2003. Add to that the silver supply/demand phenomenon, and that means far higher prices—unless they repealed the law of supply and demand when I wasn't looking.

These are just a few of the reasons why ignoring gold or silver will cost you a fortune in missed opportunities. In the worst case, gold is headed towards at least $2,500 an ounce (currently over $1,000, up from $280 so far), and silver is headed for at least $100 (currently more than $17, up from $4). And the best by far is still ahead. Long-term gold and silver investors should make as much as ten times their money—and maybe a lot more—before we get a sudden rush of brains to the head and create a sound currency.

All About Gold

Gold can be spun out into a thread that is so thin it is nearly invisible to the naked eye. It can be pounded out into a plate so thin that light can pass through it. It won't rust or corrode. It will look the same in 1,000 years as it does now.

It bonds well with other metals to form alloys of varying purity, and most of the gold ever mined is still in existence.

No other reality-based myth has been as durable as gold. We've all heard of The Golden Boy, The Pot of Gold at the End of the Rainbow, The Golden Touch, The Golden Fleece, The Golden Rule (he who has the gold makes the rules?), The Goose That Laid the Golden Eggs, and the Gold Medal for the winner. Golden engagement and wedding rings are recognized all over the world as a symbol of bonding through marriage. In India and the Middle East, gold is often melted down into jewelry and worn for security and a display of wealth.

All About Silver

Silver is the poor man's gold. Think of gold as large denomination money, and silver as small bills. A one-ounce gold coin is now worth more than $1000, but you can buy a roll of pre-1965, ninety percent silver dimes for under $60 a roll. Partly because it is so much cheaper, the potential buying pool is much larger, and industrial use is so much greater, silver will be more profitable than gold by at least one hundred percent!

Silver is by far the more important industrial metal. There are more than two thousand silver industrial applications, and Uncle Sam has zero stockpiles of silver. It can be polished to be more reflective than any other metal, which is why it is used as backing for glass to make mirrors. It has thousands of essential uses in industry. It is an essential component for the manufacture of all audio and videotape, and all film. But above all, it is routinely accepted as money, especially in India, China, and the Middle East.

And remember, silver went from under $2 to $50 in the last bull market, when the consensus was that there was many times more silver than gold above the ground. Now the ratio is reversed. There is five times more gold above ground than silver.

Born Again Gold Bug

When I did a recent radio interview, the host (who was basically friendly), said, "You've always liked gold."

My response? "No, no, no!" I have been bearish on gold for most of two decades before December 2003. I have only been bullish on gold twelve years out of the thirty-four years I have been publishing *The Ruff Times*. I was bearish or neutral for twenty-two years. I've only been bullish since December 2003. But I guess I can never shake the label of "gold bug" the media gave me way back in the '70s.

When I first began publishing *The Ruff Times* in 1975, I begged my subscribers to buy $120 gold and $2 silver. Gold finally topped out at $850, and silver went to $50. I said, "Sell!" at $750 and $35 respectively. Then for more than twenty years, I made money for *The*

Ruff Times subscribers mostly in stocks, bonds, real estate, and other traditional investments.

At the risk of sounding immodest, (Once I thought I was getting humble. It felt awful, but I was only coming down with the flu.) I probably learned at least as much about gold and silver and their markets in that bull run back then as any writer alive today.

Now I'm back again in familiar territory, riding the Golden Calf, since December 2003. As the golden calf grows into a massive bull over the next few years, you can make a ton of money in gold, more than twice as much in silver, and even a lot more than that in carefully selected mining stocks from my Investment Menu (See www.rufftimes.com).

Three Different Uses for the Precious Metals

There are serious uses for gold and silver that have little to do with investment, and gold bugs often miss that. You need to know the difference. The metals have three basic uses:

1. Gold and silver coins as personal insurance against a declining dollar.

2. Government holdings of gold backing for the currency (non-investment).

3. Gold and silver for investments *when things are right*, and only then.

Timing makes no difference with number one and number two. They are for all seasons, not for speculation or investment. However, when you want to invest in gold and silver, timing is everything.

Gold and Silver Insurance

You should always own gold and silver coins as an insurance policy. Like homeowners' or automobile insurance, its purpose is to protect you against unpredictable economic and political calamities (like now), that you always hope would never happen.

It's there to use as real money in the case of a worst-case, like an inflationary currency collapse, or terrorist hackers shutting down the power grid so no one has access to their dollars at the bank or at the ATM and they can't open the supermarket cash registers. The same terrorist-financed hackers could break into the computers of the money-center banks where most of the world's dollars are in hyperspace, insert a destructive virus, and the world's dollars would disappear in a nanosecond.

Remember, only about 5% of the world's dollars are minted, printed, or coined. The rest are only on the computers of banks. If the computer data is wiped out, there could go the monetary system of the world, because the dollar is the world's reserve currency. This could mean the instant collapse of the American economy, and maybe western civilization. Then the world would instinctively go back to gold and silver as a means of exchange and store of value until the computers are fixed and a new paper-money system is cobbled together.

These things always seemed to be unthinkable in our otherwise comfortable world, but we have never lived through a period of Obamanomics nor had such an implacable enemy as Islamo-fascism.

Insurance Action Steps

Each family should have at least one half-bag of pre-1965, commonly circulated, ninety percent "junk silver" dimes, quarters and halves (360 ounces of silver). Junk silver can be bought from any neighborhood coin dealer or from one of the recommended bullion and coin dealers in Appendix A.

Due to Obamanomics, gold and silver will explode in value and your insurance coins will become a fantastic investment, which they may not have been when you bought them. In the case of less drastic events, such as mere rising-price inflation, they will still be very profitable.

For instance, because of the critical supply/demand situation, as the holder of any form of physical silver, you will find the industries that need them will have to bid up the price until you are willing to part with yours. $100 an ounce, anyone?

Coin insurance is a buying decision for all seasons, and it only becomes an investment if bad or even mildly bad things (like slowly rising inflation) happen in the world. This is not for short-term profit, but for long-term protection.

You would really need it if a monetary crisis or a war gets bad enough and lasts long enough that we have started to universally use coins as the alternative "real" currency. It might even not take that long for merchants to get the drift. During the OPEC gas crisis in the '70s when inflation and silver were in a runaway mode and gas prices were exploding, a few enterprising gas-station operators were advertising gas for a dime a gallon—pre-1965, ninety-percent silver dimes—because a ninety-percent silver dime was worth more than the posted price-per-gallon.

Like all insurance, the coins are there to use when bad things happen which you hope won't happen. All insurance is a bet that bad things will happen. You win your bet only if you have a car crash, or a fire, or if you die. With orthodox insurance, it doesn't matter if you win or lose your bet, the premiums are gone forever. In the case of coin insurance, the premiums are still there forever and appreciating, no matter what.

Gold And Silver As Monetary Backing: A Condensed History

In theory, we should be backing our currency with gold and silver, making it fully exchangeable into the metals, like America did for almost two centuries. It's a principled cause that dedicated gold bugs should fight for, but it has nothing to do with investing in gold.

Years ago when Americans began to vote themselves benefits from the public treasury, government started to print and issue more receipts (currency) than there was gold or silver in the warehouses (which we now called "banks"). Who would know, as long as not too many holders of receipts showed up at the bank with their receipts to demand their gold or silver at the same time?

And then, we eventually thought of the paper receipt (currency) as real money all by itself.

For a long time we had confidence in the "gold and silver backing." But human nature never changes. We soon got so accustomed to our government benefits, paid with receipts (dollars), that we accepted the printing of more and more receipts (money). We were ignorant of the cause of monetary inflation. The only signs were rising prices of goods, and rising gold and silver, but most people had no idea what was really causing inflation.

The stage was finally set when it became obvious to foreign dollar-holders that there was not enough metal to meet all demands, so they began jostling to be the first in line to present dollars at "the gold window." Panic!! Nixon finally faced the reality that there soon would be more receipts (dollars) presented for redemption than there was gold available. Until then, foreign governments could exchange their dollars for gold, but we were steadily running out of gold in Fort Knox, as foreign confidence in the paper dollar had sagged so badly due to monetary inflation, that we were soon threatened with losing all our gold reserves.

So Nixon closed the "gold window" at the Federal Reserve to stem the tide, and the process was complete; the dollar was now completely detached from gold and silver, and greenbacks were now just a "fiat currency" (money just because a government order or "fiat" declared it).

Once we accepted that the horse was out of the barn, Congress no longer worried about whether we had enough gold and silver in the bank to redeem the ever-growing supply of banknotes, and the political claims on government "entitlements" were soaring. Inflation was the inevitable consequence of money creation.

Then, Uncle Sam began an anti-gold campaign to de-monetize the metal and separate it in the public mind from "money." They even began making and marketing gold and silver coins (eagles) as "mere commodities" and collectibles. However, enough of us remembered the monetary meaning of gold and silver—that they rose at the slightest threat of inflation. And as gold was an internationally traded commodity and a lot of foreigners had not bought into the U.S. anti-gold propaganda, the price began to rise.

You Can't Go Home Again

Restoring gold backing to the currency would seem to be the obvious solution. In theory, that is so, but that won't work until we are willing to forego our soaring government benefits and accept the discipline that gold and silver backing provide. We need a sudden rush of brains to the head and character to the heart—and wallet! Don't hold your breath! If you think that will happen, I have a big orange used bridge in San Francisco to sell you.

It won't happen until the present money system has totally collapsed and we have nothing to lose by replacing it with an honest hard-money system. Now, we collectively feel we have too much to lose. We have a huge vested interest in the status quo—our welfare, our Social Security, Medicare, Medicaid, our farm subsidies, etc.

Investing In Gold and Silver

How about making money with gold and silver?

Buying the metals strictly for investment purposes is not for short-term timing—but for long-term bull markets like now!

Fortunately, *now* the timing is right because the Obama government is creating dollars by the trillions.

Bad News Bulls

Gold and silver tend to do well when everything else is going to hell. Bad news can be good news indeed! When the stock market or real estate is in the grip of inflation or an inflation-induced recession or depression, gold and silver will thrive. The worse things get, the higher they will go. They are classic contrarian investments.

If the essential elements are not there, gold and silver are lousy investments, as they were for two decades. Although the very long-term prospects are just fine, the metals can be near dead for years at a time—like those two decades between the end of the last bull market in 1980 and the beginning of the current one. All the factors *are* now lined up, and will remain that way for years, perhaps forever.

In all probability, you will eventually make money in the metals in the long run, no matter when you bought them or how much you paid for them. Any investment in gold and silver now at almost any price will eventually pay off.

After 1980, when I finally got it through my thick head that the bloom was off the (golden) rose, I waited patiently (impatiently?) for two decades while gold and silver went sideways and down for many years. As it was not the right time for the metals, I made money for my subscribers in carefully selected stocks and bonds and real estate for more than two decades, while keeping an eye out for today's conditions.

A Word About Investment Attitudes

Let me digress for a moment for a brief dissertation on dysfunctional and functional investor attitudes. If you are a realistic optimist like me, you are always looking for the silver (or gold) linings in the gathering clouds, if that is reality. I just want to be right, not because my ego requires it, but because in my profession, being wrong costs me subscribers, or missed opportunities for them. True optimism includes realistically looking for opportunities among bad developments.

Gold and silver are bad-news bulls!

You won't be bullish about gold and silver if you think everything will be hunky dory in the world at large. You would have to believe in Obamanomics or that trillion-dollar bailouts have no inflationary implications, or that Social Security and Medicare will be cured without printing money.

If the world should suddenly turn sane and the metals should tube, the true optimist will cut his potential losses and look for new opportunities, as I finally did after the gold bull market of the '70s, when I finally accepted the fact that the gold bull was dead. When the current gold bull market has run its course, if the currency and the economy have hung together, we should be able to put the Wall Street Journal on the wall, throw darts at it, and invest in the holes. But for now, we must buy silver and gold until it is stock-dart time. That will probably be years from now.

Ironically, gold bugs can be just as ideologically blind as stock-brokers. Many of those who were ideologically turned on to gold because of their crusade to reinstall the gold standard, confused those things with gold's periodic merits as an investment. I had loved gold for six years in the '70s, and found it hard to turn seriously bearish in the '80s.

Lesson well learned!

Ideology is the enemy of investment, because it obscures reality. You can be a Pollyanna on gold and silver, and may be right or wrong, but not because of your optimism or pessimism. You need to be an optimist to perceive opportunity when things don't measure up to the world you would like to see, as opposed to a realistic view of the world and the markets as they really are.

A real optimist knows when to plant corn when everybody else is expecting a drought, and when not to. Although optimism and pessimism are states of mind, and have nothing to do with truth, they have a lot to do with guts—the ability to be comfortable looking north when everyone else is looking south. I may be wrong about a lot of things, but I try to be driven by realism and objective truth, not some socially approved state of mind.

Why Wall Street is Cool to the Metals

Don't be surprised if Wall Street doesn't share my enthusiasm. It is natural for brokers to be optimistically bullish on the stock market. Why? It is the source of their income—commissions.

It is also natural for them to reject bullish gold and silver forecasts, which coincide with bearish stock-market forecasts. Their clients only buy stocks when brokers say that the market is going up and those opinions may be right or wrong at any given time.

Wall Street is uniformly cool to gold and silver. They usually are either actively against it as a holding for their clients, or they act as if the precious metals don't exist. Most 401Ks ban the metals. Until the gold and silver ETFs (Exchange Traded Funds), brokers didn't make any commissions if clients decided to own some bullion. (I am nervous about bullion ETFs, as you can't be positive management has really bought the required metal backing.)

Further, mining stocks are only a tiny proportion of the stocks available to brokers. If you added up the capitalization of all the gold and silver mining stocks in the world, plus the value of all the metal available to the market and (supposedly) in ETFs, it would be less than the combined market capitalization of Microsoft and Google. A tiny bit of increased volume would bid them out of sight.

If all the brokers in the world became gold bugs or silver advocates, there wouldn't be even close to enough merchandise to accommodate them, so their pessimism about the metals is easy to understand, as measured against their self-interest. But it has *nothing* to do with reality!

Conditions Favorable to Investing in Gold and Silver

So if timing is everything, what conditions make gold and silver good investments?

1. **Money-creation** (monetary inflation) must be in a long-term upward trend. Obamanomics has made it so.

2. **The dollar losing exchange value against foreign currencies**. This is so essential, that I finally turned bullish when the dollar began its recent decline when I did the final edits on a book in December 2003. Without a weakening dollar on the exchange markets, any moves in the metals will be temporary. Now we have moved beyond that into the next currency phase —the metals rising against *all* currencies, which is immensely bullish.

3 **War or the prospect of war.** The wars in Iraq and Afghanistan are beginning to meet this condition, although the shooting has

been contained locally, mostly to the Middle East. War breaking out further into the world—a terrorist nuclear, biological or computer-system attack, or Iranian fanatics nuking Tel Aviv—would meet this requirement. We're on the brink, but not there yet. War is a wild card because it triggers inflation due to wartime spending and national and international fear, and is basically unpredictable.

Not *all* three conditions have to be met at the same time to make gold and silver good investments, but conditions one and two are essential. War would help a lot. Wait a minute—that sounds perverse!

The Right Strategy

What is the proper strategy for long-term investors in bullion and coins? Simple. Buy bullion or coins, take them home, hide them, be patient, and wait out the declines—or treat those temporary declines as opportunities to buy more. I lust after those retreats. I will be marketing *The Ruff Times* for a few more years and I want to get new subscribers into gold and silver as cheaply as possible.

When all commodities are in a bull market, gold and silver are the only commodities that are practical for the typical middle-class American. Unlike zinc or copper or steel or soybeans, you don't have to take on a lot of risk, like a leveraged futures contract, or have a truck back up to your door and dump a pile of copper on your porch. You don't need a warehouse to store your gold or silver. You can simply go to your corner coin dealer, or call our recommended dealers (see Appendix A), pay cash, and take it home, or simply buy it in the ground—as gold or silver mining stock—like any other stock.

With mining stocks and gold mutual funds, you only have to watch one fundamental—the price of the metals. When they go up, all the mining stocks go up. When the wind blows, even the turkeys fly. Of course, some will fly higher than others for fundamental reasons: production, property potential, management, sufficient capital, etc. My job is to help you pick the best (see www.rufftimes.com).

The Futures Pitfall

Don't buy gold and silver futures. If you buy a futures contract for any commodity, including gold or silver, you are highly leveraged, and a comparatively small decline can wipe out your "margin," and your broker will then give you perhaps the only free advice he will ever give you: a margin call! You will have to put up more margin money, or you will be liquidated, and there goes your money.

Gold and silver are dangerous *only* if you are thinking short-term or in leveraged volatile instruments, like futures contracts. If you have physical gold or silver or fully owned mining stocks, you just wait it out, or use the dips to buy more. Declines are great opportunities.

I will never buy gold or silver futures. The only times I did that over the years, I got my head (and my empty wallet) handed to me. I don't have the temperament or the time to continually watch the computer screen to be a short-term trader. Amateur futures traders get killed over and over again, until they are broke or just give up.

Even today, I will sometimes meet someone who says, "Howard, I saw you on TV, so I took your advice in the '70s and bought gold and lost a lot of money. I'll never listen to you again." Invariably, upon further questioning, he admits he bought gold futures and got caught in a short-term correction. I never told anyone to buy gold or silver futures for the above reasons. And he didn't subscribe to *The Ruff Times*, so he didn't know when I said to sell.

Avoid futures contracts, unless you are a very quick-on-your feet trader who is prepared to accept some big losses to balance against the profits you may make later. And never meet a margin call!

And don't try to day-trade the mining stocks. This is a very dangerous market for futures speculators and day traders. In the bull market of the '70s, I saw retreats as much as 30 percent along the way to the eventual huge profits. A correction could wipe out futures traders in minutes.

Exchange-traded Funds (ETFs)

I'm especially dubious about SLV and GLD. There is no way to be positive that Barclays, which owns SLV, is really using your purchase of SLV stock to buy the promised silver backing. In the current cash crisis, selling shares of SLV and not buying the metal may meet their serious need for cash, and Barclays is cash short. I can't prove this, but human nature and their self-interest make me nervous.

Gold and Silver—What and Where to Buy

When you do leave the herd, where will you buy your precious metals? You can either go to the firms I recommend in Appendix A of this book (I only recommend six because at my age I'm too tired to monitor more, although I am sure there are other good ones). Or you can go to your local coin dealer.

There is one basic rule—*always compare prices*. They can vary dramatically from dealer to dealer and from hour to hour, even with my recommended firms.

What kind of metals should you buy?

1) **"Junk silver."** Start here. These are pre-1965 dimes, dollars and halves sold by the bag. Price is determined by their silver value; it has nothing to do with the face value. A bag is approximately 715 ounces, but you can also buy a half bag. Everyone investing in metals should start there. I suggest you have as much as a bag for each member of your family. If that's too much for your pocketbook, do what you can, even if it's just a roll of 90-percent silver dimes.

2) **Gold and silver coins** which are bought, sold, and priced strictly for their metal content. There is a big variety of gold and silver coins available on the market. I like bullion coins like krugerrands, eagles, or any of the popular internationally accepted coins. Remember that the value of gold coins is several times higher than silver coins, so think of gold-bullion coins as $100 bills and silver coins as small change. (Is that what Obama meant when he promised "change"?) You need a variety of both.

3) **Silver rounds,** coin-like silver or gold tokens that are created by some dealers. You will pay the bullion value plus a small premium.

After you have accumulated a few thousand dollars worth of the above, if you have money left over (many of you will not) you can look at mining stocks. Gold and silver mining stocks fit into several categories, from big "Blue Chip" producers, clear down to "holes in the ground surrounded by liars."

The most money in gold stocks will be made over the years by investors in gold Exploration Companies. The stock market might collapse, in which case you may find no place to exchange your mining stocks into dollars until the market reestablishes itself, so be cautious, with a bias towards the physical metals.

4) There are **bullion bars**, ranging from one hundred to one thousand ounces. If you buy bars and take them home, however, and you want to sell them, they will have to be assayed with additional costs, and probably insured. I am not as interested in them. I prefer coins, which need no assay.

Other Stock Industry Groups

In addition to gold and silver, there are other inflation-related investments I like. For example, as inflation picks up and the price of oil rises back over $100 per barrel, there will be great opportunities in oil-service companies. I don't trust the producers, like Exxon, as much as I once did, but the companies that build and service the oil rigs (like *Schlumberger* (SLB) and *Halliburton* (HAL) will have all the business they can handle. Eventually, the political tide will turn in that direction. As long as the stock market is functioning, they make sense.

I also like *Canadian Oil Income Trusts*. They buy oil production and pay you a dividend based on their profit. Because the Canadian government has given them a break so they don't have to pay corporate taxes, they have high dividends, sometimes *as much as 25 percent*.

When the price of oil came down, these stocks suffered big time, and some had to cut their dividends. But as oil goes up, they will be back in business again.

The Canadian government has decided that giving them a tax break costs the government money, so they have ruled that these companies now have to pay corporate taxes, which, of course, cut their dividends dramatically. But they grandfathered the existing ones. I especially like those that were grandfathered for another year or two.

Contact *Jim Raby* at *National Securities* at 800-431-4488 or 206-343-6225. He's my broker.

Nuclear Power and Uranium Mining

As the price of gas goes up, there will be a growing trend towards *nuclear power*. The environmentalists who have fought against it will suddenly have a rush of brains to the head when they finally have to acknowledge that nuclear power plants don't contribute to their big bugaboo—alleged "global warming."

There are thirty-five nuclear plants on the drawing board or under construction right now. There is only about half enough uranium above ground to meet their needs. So I like *uranium mining stocks*.

How About Real Estate?

I am often asked, "When will it be time to buy real estate again." An old adage says, "Never try to catch a falling safe." The Wall Street variation is "never try to catch a falling knife."

Real estate is still in decline, and there is still a huge overhang of foreclosed and unsold properties. Until these have been worked through and the market has rebalanced itself, residential and commercial real estate will not bottom out.

If you want to buy a home to live in, you can probably find a great deal on a foreclosed home at today's low mortgage rates. However, avoid residential real estate for investment or speculation for a while longer. Inflation hedges only make sense if they have an upside. At these prices, the upside of real estate is a long ways away, if not non-existent. I will recommend real estate as an inflation hedge eventually, but not yet. I'll let you know in *The Ruff Times* when the time is right.

www.rufftimes.com

Acknowledgements

My book is not the product of a one-man band.

Several people played major parts in this production.

First, there is Ellen Reid, The Book Shepherd, whose job it is to prepare it for publication. She found the book designer who could give the book a very polished look and create the dramatic cover. She respected the fact that I am an experienced writer but didn't pull any punches.

Mireille Koester was more than a skilled editor. Even an experienced writer needs a good editor; one who can find all the things that were overlooked. During her college years, Mireille lived in our home. That is where she met her husband who was in our home recovering from a broken foot. Mireille was not just an editor, she was a fan. She knew how to edit without changing my voice. I have had numerous battles with editors who wanted to make me sound more like Wall Street than Howard Ruff. Mireille caught the spirit of it, and I accepted most of her suggestions.

My wife, Kay, tolerated my obsession of writing the book while writing her own personal history. She provided a nurturing environment for me while I spent four or five hours a day reading and researching, and then more hours going through numerous drafts.

Last, but by far not least, is Joann Allen. Joann has been my faithful assistant for almost 30 years. She has the technical computer skills I don't have. Whenever I get in trouble technically passing drafts back and forth, I would call Joann and she somehow would find a way to fix it. Kari Crane, who manages our contacts with subscribers, also provided crucial input.

My staff are long-term friends, as close to me as my own offspring. For them, I give deep and heart-felt thanks.

Without their help, this book could not have been written. The older I get, the harder it is to write a book. But just because there is snow on the roof doesn't mean the fire is out in the furnace. I still have a passion to teach middle-class people on "Main Street" to find investment profits that Wall Street ignores in hard times.

And then there are my faithful Ruff Times subscribers. I will say "thanks" by helping them make a pot full of money in the age of Obamanomics.

Valuable Sources of Information

A. What I Read

*T*he Wall Street Journal: Everyone should read *The Wall Street Journal*. Its editorials are the best to be found anywhere. The statistical information regarding money supply and markets, and some of the "think pieces" on the front and back pages are invaluable. It should be scanned every day.

When I read it, I look for the feature articles on the front page, the op-eds and the editorials on the back three pages, then turn to the commodities section about two-thirds of the way through. Anyone who wants to protect his assets and does not read *The Wall Street Journal* is foolish.

Business Week, and **Fortune:** I wade through all these magazines as soon as they hit my desk. *Business Week* is a very conservative, somewhat sober, but generally quite accurate analysis of what's going on in the world. I have found a lot of key pieces of data from which very important decisions have been made.

Forbes: Even though it has been wrong in many of its editorial conclusions, is a useful source of data. Just ignore their generally anti-hard money stance. They declared gold dead when it was $110 an ounce, so they are not very objective about gold and silver, but it's still well worth reading.

Time and *Newsweek:* These are the standard news magazine. I don't read them for opinion. I read them for information and then I apply my own standard of judgment as to how objective they are. Their liberal bias is considerable, but sometimes I find them useful when I need to know how the liberal press thinks, and everyone should read them with appropriate skepticism.

B. Advisory Newsletters

The Ruff Times. 51 West Center, Suite 519, Orem, UT 84057; www.rufftimes.com; You can subscribe online on my website.

Richard Russell's *Dow Theory Letter.* Written by a wise old pro. An *indispensable* source of market information. P.O. Box 1759, La Jolla, CA 92038; www.dowtheoryletter.com.

Casey Research www.caseyresearch.com; 800-528-0559; P. O. Box 84900, Phoenix, AZ 85071. Doug Casey is a very savvy and entertaining writer with an encyclopedic knowledge of mines and metals. We have often tangled on values, but never on investments.

The Aden Forecast by Pamela and Mary Anne Aden. www.adenforecast.com; P. O. Box 79026, St. Louis, MO 63179. They are also old timers, and their regular newsletter is clear and complete, technical but readable, and always right (they agree with me). They are great gals and terrific friends.

The Silver Investor Report by David Morgan. www.silver-investor. com; 509-464-1651; 21307 Buckeye Lake, Colbert WA 99005

Jay Taylor's *Gold and Technology Report* www.miningstocks. com; P. Bo Box 871, Woodside NY 11377. Jay Taylor is a new friend with a towering reputation.

Human Events www.humaneventsonline.com 800-787-7557; One Masachussetts Ave, NW, Washington, D.C. 20001. A must-read weekly paper for politically concerned conservatives.

The McAlvany Intelligence Advisor by Don McAlvany www.mcalvany.com. 800-525-9556; 166 Turner Drive, Durango, CO 81303. A good guy and a recommended coin dealer.

The Dines Letter by Jim Dines, The Original Gold (now "Uranium") Bug. www.dinesletter.com; 800-845-8259; P. O. Box 22, Belvedere, CA 94920. An old friend and a most entertaining writer and speaker. Another must read!

Resource Opportunities by Lawrence Roulston. www.resource opportunities.com; 877-773-7677; 800 West Pender Street, Suite 1510, Vancouver, BC, Canada. Lawrence is sound and thorough.

Forecast & Strategies by Mark Skousen. www.mskousen.com 800-211-7661, One Massachusetts Avenue, Washington, D.C. 20001

C. Indispensible Information Websites

www.rufftimes.com Both free articles and paid-subscription information.

www.kitco.com A major recommended coin and bullion dealer, and a source of up-to-minute gold and silver quotes and lots of other info. I have frequent articles on their website.

www.321gold.com Great articles on the subject. I may from time to time have an article there.

www.321energy.com From the same source. Oil stocks and alternative-energy info.

www.jsmineset.com From Jim Sinclair, one of the old-timers, and a very successful (and rich) writer since the '70s.

www.silverstockreport.com Jason Hommel's Silver Stock Report.

www.thebullandbear.com Great information on gold, silver and other markets.

D. Precious Metals Dealers

KITCO: www.kitco.com; 877-775-4826; 178 West service Road, Champion, NY 12919. My regular source of up-to-the-minute gold and silver quotes.

Investment Rarities Inc., www.investmentrarities.com; 800-328-1860; 7850 Metro Highway, Minneapolis, MN 55425. Friends for 30 years.

International Collectors Associates www.mcalvany.com; 800-525-9556; 166 Turner Drive, Durango, CO 81303. McAlvany is a really good guy.

Camino Coin, www.camino.com; 800-348-8001; 851 Burlway, Suite 202, Burlingame, CA 94010.

David Hall Rare Coins www.davidhall.com; 800-759-7575; P. O. Box 6220, Newport Beach, CA 92658.

Rocklin Coin Shop (Jason Hommel) www.silverstockreport. com; 530-913-4359 or 530-913-0553; 480 Granite Drive, Rocklin, CA 95677.

E. Food Storage

Preparedness Plus (800-588-5412); www.preparednessplus.net. (Enter "Howard Ruff" on the coupon-redemption code at check out for a special discount.)

Emergency Essentials (800-999-1863); www.beprepared.com. (Enter "Ruff" on the coupon-redemption code at check out for a special one-time discount.)

You can buy everything there from your emergency kit to a full year's supply of food.

Martens Health and Survival (800-824-7861); www.marten survival.com.

Karen Varner (801-225-0948). Email her at your72hourkitlady@ yahoo.com. Karen has worked with my subscribers for a number of years. Contact her to learn where the sales are. She has coordinated group discounts, and gives free advice. She will walk you through your specific needs; pick her brain.

F. Survival And Technology

Making the Best of Basics: Family Preparedness Handbook, by James Talmage Stevens. This is the best-selling book ever on basic storage programs for everyday necessities. Available in most book stores.

Websites for emergency planning: www.ready.gov and www.redcross.org. http://www.orem.org/index.php?option=com_content&task=view&id=301&Itemid=286 is one of my local community websites that has terrific information on emergency preparation.

G. Vitamins, Minerals And Protein

Hi-Q Nutrition Brain Food, Manufactured by Howard Ruff (877-665-6818). www.hiqnutrition.com.

Neo Life: Norvel & Joann Martens. (800-824-7861); www.marten survival.com. I've done business with them for 25 years.

H. Gold Mining Stockbroker

National Securities, James Raby, www.nationalsecurities.com; 800 431-4488; 1001 Fourth Avenue, 22nd Floor, Seattle, WA 98154. My broker. An honest source of info on mining stocks for his clients. Trades Canadian and U.S. stocks.

APPENDIX B

Investment Menu Shopping Suggestions

The following are the headings for the list of recommended investments which are regularly included and updated in *The Ruff Times*. Visit our website at www.rufftimes.com to subscribe. You will see the list of specific stocks in each issue.

– *Oil Service Companies*

– *Investing For Income*

– *Investing For Capital Gains in a Bear Market*

– *Gold Mining Mutual Funds*

– *Blue Chips: Major Gold Producers and Second-Tier Producers*

– *Development Companies*

– *Exploration Companies*

– *Pure Silver Plays*

– *Combination Plays*

– *Uranium: Producing Companies*

– *Junior Uranium Developments*

– *Uranium Exploration Companies*

– *Copper Mining*

If you are interested in mining stocks, call Jim Raby at National Securities at 800-431-4488 or 206-343-6225. He's my broker.

---

www.rufftimes.com